CONTEMPORARY COMPROMISE

STANDING FOR TRUTH IN AN AGE OF DECEPTION

JOHN GOETSCH

First published in 2010 by Striving Together Publications, a ministry of Lancaster Baptist Church, Lancaster, CA 93535. Striving Together Publications is committed to providing tried, trusted, and proven books that will further equip local churches to carry out the Great Commission. Your comments and suggestions are valued.

Striving Together Publications
4020 E. Lancaster Blvd.
Lancaster, CA 93535
800.201.7748

Cover design by Andrew Jones
Layout by Craig Parker
Edited by Cary Schmidt
Special thanks to our proofreaders.

ISBN 978-1-59894-105-0

Printed in the United States of America

CONTENTS

The contemporary church and its theology are changing rapidly. These changes, in both theology and practice, are alarming to any committed Bible student and Christian. While the emergent church is attracting thousands of followers, its message is increasingly unbiblical and man-centered.

In the midst of these trends away from truth, *Contemporary Compromise* calls us back to the anchor of biblical authority and absolute truth. In these pages, Dr. John Goetsch clearly exposes the error of present day, pop-culture Christianity and challenges us all to hold fast to the faith "*once delivered.*" There are several things I greatly appreciate about this book:

The Author. Dr. John Goetsch is a man with a heart for God and a love for people. As I labor with him in the ministry of West Coast Baptist College, I watch him expend himself in the trenches of daily ministry and personal mentoring. The principles he shares in this book flow from a life engaged in the cause of personal discipleship and life-transformation.

The Spirit. I love the humble sincerity of Dr. Goetsch's spirit in these pages. He has taken a very difficult subject, applied the Word of God, and delivered a strong admonition with a spirit of kindness. While these pages could, in some sense, be viewed as a rebuke to Christians who are compromising, in truth they read more like a plea for Christians to return to and stand strong upon the truth of God's Word. There is not a hint of condescension or arrogance in this volume. The pure heart of a good man of God flows from these pages.

The Truth. Dr. Goetsch says what needs to be said. He exposes the error and stands upon truth. He backs up his conclusions with the authority of God's Word. Throughout this book, Scripture speaks for itself. If you will read with an open heart, God's Word will strengthen your faith.

The Results. The life and ministry of Dr. Goetsch stand as a tremendous witness, validating the truth of these pages. The steadfast life is a life worth living! The results of heeding the cautions and challenges of this book will simply be that your soul and life will be anchored to a fixed position in Jesus Christ. Decades of faithfulness to God's truth will bear the wonderful harvest of an authentic, fruitful Christian life and ministry.

I believe *Contemporary Compromise* is more needed than ever before. I pray that you will read with an open heart and that God's Holy Spirit will do a great work in your life through these pages. May God strengthen you to remain *"stedfast, unmoveable, always abounding in the work of the Lord"* until He comes again!

Sincerely,

Paul Chappell
Pastor

INTRODUCTION

When I started in the ministry in 1974, I never thought I would write. When I started writing in 2001, I never thought I would write on this subject. As a means of communication, I often prefer writing. A quick memo, email, or text is a reliable way to give instruction, ask a question, or pass along important information. In today's world of technology we can send a written message quickly and absolve ourselves of any further responsibility. We don't have to wait for a response, answer any additional questions, or debate the matter. Over and done; out of my hair; off my "to do list"—I can write it, send it, and forget it!

The problem with written communication in contrast to face to face communication is that the person receiving the message cannot discern the spirit or heart in which it is given.

For years I have taught speech and homiletics students that you cannot separate the messenger from the message. The conduit is as important as the content. No one wants to drink water from an old garden hose! We tend to read with eagerness a message from a friend or loved one whom we know well, whereas we read more skeptically a letter from someone we've never met.

Thus, preaching for me is a whole lot easier than writing. I could be happy if all God allowed me to do is preach, as it would be far more than I deserve to do for Him. When preaching, I feel as if I can discern the mood and attitude of the audience and communicate accordingly. The audience likewise can sense my spirit and heart as a preacher and listen accordingly. As I write however, you cannot see my facial expressions or hear my voice inflection or discern my body language. You only have "black marks" on a page in front of you, and the influence they have is limited to the words and punctuation I choose.

The Apostle Paul was used by God to write several of our New Testament books. The book of Romans contains a tremendous amount of doctrine that was essential for early Christians to understand. I believe Paul was fully aware that he was being guided by the Holy Spirit to pen each word and had full confidence that God would make each of them count. However, it is interesting as he opens the book that he makes known to the readers that he longs to preach to them in person what he is about to write to them in the letter.

> *First, I thank my God through Jesus Christ for you all,*
> *that your faith is spoken of throughout the whole world.*
> *For God is my witness, whom I serve with my spirit*

in the gospel of his Son, that without ceasing I make mention of you always in my prayers; Making request, if by any means now at length I might have a prosperous journey by the will of God to come unto you. For I long to see you, that I may impart unto you some spiritual gift, to the end ye may be established; That is, that I may be comforted together with you by the mutual faith both of you and me. Now I would not have you ignorant, brethren, that oftentimes I purposed to come unto you, (but was let hitherto,) that I might have some fruit among you also, even as among other Gentiles. I am debtor both to the Greeks, and to the Barbarians; both to the wise, and to the unwise. So, as much as in me is, I am ready to preach the gospel to you that are at Rome also.—ROMANS 1:8–15

Paul knew that what he was writing was absolutely true— inspired by a holy God! But he longed to preach it to them. Why? Because he knew in preaching he could communicate so much better face to face the message than with mere written words. The message had changed him, and now he was a part of that message he preached.

Now before we go any further, please understand this: nothing on the pages in front of you is inspired other than the Word of God (and I will try to use it often). But I would rather communicate much of what is on my heart in person than in a book, because I really would like you to be able to discern my heart. I am not interested in spiritual politics or endless debates over non-essentials. I have worked hard for over thirty-five years

XII   CONTEMPORARY COMPROMISE

to stay out of those arenas. But I am concerned about Truth—and I speak here of absolute Truth—which God has given us in His Word to guide us individually and ecclesiastically.

During the Leadership Conference in July of 2009, my pastor, Dr. Paul Chappell called me to his office one afternoon. Quite frankly, over these years we have had only a handful of these one-on-one conversations. As my pastor, I listen to him preach, labor alongside of him in the ministry, and try to discern his heart and the direction God has given him for our ministry. We have an outstanding relationship, and I delight in serving under him at Lancaster Baptist Church and West Coast Baptist College.

As we chatted casually there in his office, he expressed his concern over the direction that some of the young men in our movement were heading. We spoke of some of our own graduates who were being influenced by new-evangelical books and blogs. I sensed the burden he was carrying on his shoulders for these young men in particular and even some of the more seasoned preachers who seemed swayed by the "winds" of compromise. As he spoke, my mind raced across the country to cities, churches, and schools where once I had enjoyed preaching as an evangelist but now could not return because of changes that had been made.

Pastor suggested that we should devote some chapels in the upcoming school year to address some of the issues that were pulling our young men away from the fundamental Truths of God's Word. He asked me to look at the chapel schedule and see if there might be a week where we could move some things around in order to address this topic for several days. Perhaps it could even develop into some kind of conference to help our students and others understand the issues and how the Bible addresses them.

As he spoke, I thought back to when I was in college. I shared with Pastor how Dr. B. Myron Cedarholm at Maranatha Baptist Bible College would take three weeks every spring and talk about the history of fundamentalism and the dangers of new-evangelicalism. He would tell us stories about Billy Graham's decision to include Catholic priests on his platforms and other compromises of that era. We practically had those sermons memorized by the time we were seniors. While I didn't appreciate them much then, I was glad that someone had taken the time to warn me and keep my focus on Truth rather than trends.

I told Pastor it was a great idea, and promised that I would check the schedule before I left town. My first question was: "Pastor, who would you like to bring in to help us with this? Do you have someone in mind?" He sat there and just stared at me. My mind was racing to think of some "old" veteran we could bring in and relive for us the last century of our movement. Unfortunately, most everyone I thought of was with the Lord! I said, "Pastor, perhaps you and I could do some preaching on it." He just stared at me. Finally, he said, "Just think about it."

I did think about it. I thought about it a lot over the next several weeks. I emailed him within the next few days with a week on the schedule that I thought might work to address this subject. I suggested several speakers. I even had a cool name for the conference and how we could promote it on campus among our students! I never heard back from him.

As the semester unfolded, it turned out that through some cancellations, there were some extra slots in the chapel schedule that needed to be filled. I normally preach once a week, but there were some weeks now where I had two slots and even one week with three. Since I hadn't heard from Pastor I decided to develop and preach at least an introductory message on the subject. As I started, I announced that I wasn't sure that I would be able to finish the message in one chapel as I wanted to share my heart and express my concern for our students and the future of God's people. I didn't get very far into the message that day—in fact, it took me three chapels to get through that one message.

The response by our students was startling to me. Many stopped over the next weeks to thank me for preaching on the topic. Others sent emails encouraging me to take additional chapels and help them. Some of them as newer Christians were grateful for the information and warning while others expressed how the messages were helping them understand "why" they were a fundamental Baptist. The more I studied and prepared, the more I wanted to preach on the topic and try to help these eager students. Not surprisingly, I again found how relevant the Bible is to the problems of our day.

As others heard about the series they encouraged me to put some things in writing. While reluctant due to the facts stated earlier, I am going to give it my best shot and trust that the Lord will help you to know my heart.

In dealing with the subject of compromise or change it is impossible to be comprehensive. There is no way to be exhaustive or complete because the minute I stop typing, the devil will unveil a new scheme. But there is Someone who never changes and He has given us Something that is "forever settled." As I did with the students, I will endeavor to do for you—that is, I will attempt to show you principles from God's Word to help you position yourself accordingly no matter what the devil throws your way over your lifetime.

Included in this book are two valuable appendixes by Pastor Chappell to show local church application in resisting contemporary compromise. Originally published in *The Saviour Sensitive Church*, these appendixes contrast biblical ministry with man-centered ministry and provide a true color picture of the philosophy and practice of a local church that honors Christ.

As the preachers of old used to say when questions would arise: *"To the law and to the testimony: if they speak not according to this word, it is because there is no light in them"* (Isaiah 8:20).

ONE

THE THINKING
CHANGE BEGINS WITH ATTITUDES
NOT ACTIONS

For as he thinketh in his heart, so is he.
—PROVERBS 23:7A

A s a preacher, one of the real joys of being in the ministry is the opportunity to be around other preachers. As a boy I used to think preachers were from another planet—almost inhuman in a sense. I assumed the only thing they ever thought about or talked about was the Bible. I was pleasantly surprised to discover later in life that they were real people who were certainly godly but were also human. Pastors, evangelists, and missionaries are real people who enjoy life and a variety of interests. Their conversations can be downright hilarious at times as they share their experiences of a life working with people.

However, preachers do share a common burden for God's work and have a keen insight into the "state of the union" if you please. Like the children of Issachar in 1 Chronicles 12:32, they have an *"...understanding of the times."* Those who have been around for awhile sense the current trends and can accurately compare them to previous times and more importantly to the Scripture.

A FEARFUL PREDICTION

A short while back I was sitting with a group of such men. All were leaders in various fields of ministry around the world and I have a great respect for all of them. In the midst of the conversation, one of them remarked that "everything has shelf-life." In the context of the discussion I knew immediately what he meant. History shows that ministries rarely stay true to their founding principles with the same fervor for more than a generation or two.

When the statement was made I immediately resisted it in my spirit and tried to refute it in my mind. Why, I thought, do we have to resign ourselves to believe that everything changes? Why do ministries and the people in them emerge for "such a time as this" and then after years or even decades of impact fade into insignificance or even extinction? I can understand all of the reasons why they do: change of leadership, unprepared transitions, peer pressure, economic crises, and pragmatism. But why does it "have" to happen?

GOD'S MAKE UP DOESN'T CHANGE

The Bible is emphatically clear that God does not change! It's hard to misunderstand Malachi 3:6a, *"For I am the Lord, I change* not." Hebrews 13:8 states, *"Jesus Christ the same yesterday, and to day, and for ever."* The Holy Spirit then goes on to admonish us in the next verse: *"Be not carried about with divers and strange doctrines. For it is a good thing that the heart be established with grace"* (Hebrews 13:9A). The psalmist compares the changeless Creator to the changing creation in Psalm 102:25–27, *"Of old hast thou laid the foundation of the earth: and the heavens are the work of thy hands. They shall perish, but thou shalt endure: yea, all of them shall wax old like a garment; as a vesture shalt thou change them, and they shall be changed: But thou art the same, and thy years shall have no end."* So the God we serve is immutable, constant, and eternal!

GOD'S MESSAGE DOESN'T CHANGE

The message that God has commanded us to deliver to the world is also unchangeable. Do you really think that God carefully inspired the Bible with the desire that it would change with the generations? The Bible itself refutes such thinking and declares itself to be timeless. Three times in Psalm 119 the Holy Spirit is emphatic: *"For ever, O LORD, thy word is settled in heaven"* (verse 89), *"Concerning thy testimonies, I have known of old that thou hast founded them for ever"* (verse 152), *"Thy word is true from the beginning: and every one of thy righteous judgments endureth for*

THEREFORE, MY BELOVED BRETHREN, BE YE STEDFAST, UNMOVEABLE, ALWAYS ABOUNDING IN THE WORK OF THE LORD, FORASMUCH AS YE KNOW THAT YOUR LABOUR IS NOT IN VAIN IN THE LORD.

1 CORINTHIANS 15:58

ever" (verse 160). Isaiah adds: *"The grass withereth, the flower fadeth: but the word of our God shall stand for ever"* (Isaiah 40:8). The Apostle Peter enlarges on that thought in 1 Peter 1:23–25, *"Being born again, not of corruptible seed, but of incorruptible, by the word of God, which liveth and abideth for ever. For all flesh is as grass, and all the glory of man as the flower of grass. The grass withereth, and the flower thereof falleth away: But the word of the Lord endureth for ever. And this is the word which by the gospel is preached unto you."*

GOD'S MEN ARE CHANGING

God's makeup does not change. God's message does not change. So why do God's men change? Are we not also commanded to be *"stedfast"* and *"unmoveable"* in 1 Corinthians 15:58? There is no doubt that the world and culture around us is changing. The Bible says that it will! *"But evil men and seducers shall wax worse and worse, deceiving, and being deceived"* (2 Timothy 3:13). But what does Paul earnestly exhort the young preacher Timothy to do in the light of this change? *"But continue thou in the things which thou hast learned and hast been assured of, knowing of whom thou hast learned them"* (verse 14).

Would you say that alcohol is more available today than it was in the early part of the twentieth century? Would you say that it is more of a problem today than it was then? Are more lives lost each year now than back then? Are more young people out partying and ruining their futures because of alcohol now than when our grandparents lived? The answers are obvious. Yet, you could hardly find a sermon preached by Evangelist Billy Sunday where he did not "go off" against booze. The same was true of Bob Jones, Sr. These men probably had more to do with the prohibition in this country than anyone else. But today, we have prominent preachers in the pulpits of so called good churches and schools that say it's okay to have a social drink and have twisted the Scriptures to try to convince us that the Bible condones such behavior!

Should I mention Hollywood and the movie industry? Has it somehow gotten better in the last fifty years? What about music, or dress, or our language? What about the way we worship in our church services? What about the Bible we use, or the methods of ministry we practice? Is our attitude toward marriage and the family changing? Do we suddenly need secular education and approval by wicked men in order to be properly enlightened and credible? Do words like "saved" or "Baptist" or "fundamental" need to be dropped because they are offensive to a culture that is already at enmity with God? Do we need to soften our stand and blend our beliefs so that we don't offend the enemies of God?

The standard for the child of God is not the world. Most Christians today have the world as their benchmark of how to live. They look at the culture around them and say, "Well, I'm not like them." I don't go to "those" places or listen to "that" kind of music. As churches and preachers, we compare ourselves to other churches and preachers and say, "We haven't gone that far." With the world as your standard, you can just keep your distance from the world and move right along with them! You can brag about being separate from the world, but after a generation or so, you have moved miles away from God.

Let me illustrate this point more clearly. Let's say that the city of New York represents God. The world has never been like God so let's let the city of Pittsburgh represent the world. As a Christian, I'm supposed to be like Christ, so I'm over in New York with God—many miles from Pittsburgh. But

YOUR FOCUS WILL DETERMINE YOUR FOOTSTEPS.

the world is changing as we have already seen from Scripture and it's not moving closer to God but rather away from Him. So in time, the world has moved over to Chicago. Many a child of God decides to move with the world—oh they won't be just like the world, but move in that direction and before long as the world moves to Chicago, the Christian moves to Pittsburgh. By the time the world gets to Denver, the Christian is in Chicago. By the time the world has dropped off into the Pacific Ocean the child of God has bought a house in Vegas! And the whole time we pride ourselves that we are not like the world. The problem is—God is still in New York!

A FIXED POSITION

This problem has been around for a long time. Solomon of old gives wise counsel to his son in Proverbs 4:20–27, *"My son, attend to my words; incline thine ear unto my sayings. Let them not depart from thine eyes; keep them in the midst of thine heart. For they are life unto those that find them, and health to all their flesh. Keep thy heart with all diligence; for out of it are the issues of life. Put away from thee a froward mouth, and perverse lips put far from thee. Let thine eyes look right on, and let thine eyelids look straight before thee. Ponder the path of thy feet, and let all thy ways be established. Turn not to the right hand nor to the left: remove thy foot from evil."* Your focus will determine your footsteps.

As I grew up on the farm, my dad allowed me to operate a lot of machinery at a very early age. I don't really remember when I learned to drive a tractor. Dad carefully taught me to respect that equipment and be aware of the dangers. I loved working out in the fields baling hay or cultivating corn. As a little boy of four or five I would ride the fender of the tractor with my dad watching closely to see how each task was done. The first work in the field every spring however, was plowing. I was always anxious and couldn't wait for the snow to melt and the ground to dry out enough so that we could turn that soil over and begin the planting process.

One day when I was about eight or nine, my dad told me to get the tractor and pull the plow out of the shed. As I filled the tractor with fuel, Dad carefully shot grease into the axles of that plow and checked all of the parts to make sure all were in good working order. We then drove out to a square twenty-acre field and parked about halfway down on one side. Dad slid out of the seat and over to the opposite fender and said, "You're going to drive!" Wow! This was the highlight of my farming career! I was going to plow the field!

I had learned early on to listen carefully to all of the instructions that my father would give me. He said: "Now son, it is very important that you get the first furrow across this field absolutely straight. Everything else we do for the rest of the season in this field will be determined by this first furrow.

Do you understand?" As I nodded affirmatively, he said: "How are you going to do that?" I really didn't know. I had watched him plow and had ridden with him dozens of times. I knew his furrows were always straight but I had no idea how he accomplished that task.

I shrugged my shoulders, saying "I don't know." He got off the tractor and told me to take the driver's seat. "Now look over the top of the tractor to the other end of the field," he said. "What do you see?" "Nothing," was my response." "What do you see at the end of the field? Do you see a fence line?" "Yes," I stated. "Look straight ahead of the tractor and pick out one of the fence posts. Do you have one?" "Yes," was my reply. Dad then emphatically said: "Don't take your eyes off of that fence post. I'm going to walk away, but you keep your eyes on that fence post. Keep one hand on the steering wheel; push the clutch down with your foot; put the tractor in gear; and begin to move forward, but don't take your eye off that fence post. As you start moving, reach back and pull the cord behind you to trip the plow, but don't take your eye off that fence post. Okay?" I said, "Yes, sir." He added: "Now the dog will bark, and a bird may fly by, and the neighbor may drive down the road and honk his horn and wave, but don't take your eye off that fence post! Go!"

I pushed down the clutch, put the tractor in gear, eased out the clutch, reached back and tripped the plow which engaged those plowshares down into the soft earth, adjusted the throttle, and moved forward across that field with my eye fixed on that fencepost. You know what? The dog did bark—more than once, and two birds flew over, and the neighbor did drive by and honk his horn, but I kept my eye on that fencepost! My future depended on it! When I got to the other end of that field and turned the tractor around, I paused and looked back to where my dad was standing. The furrow was as straight as an arrow! I saw from a distance my dad giving me the "thumbs up" as he walked back to the barn. I learned a powerful truth that day— not just about farming—but about life.

A GLANCING AWAY

If we are going to "stay straight" we must set our attention on a fixed position. Too many people today are allowing themselves to look at that which is moving around them. Satan's dogs will yelp; the buzzards of false doctrine will fly by; and the neighboring churches will sound their tinkling cymbals, but we must keep our eyes on a fixed position, which happens to be on a Person. *"Looking unto Jesus the author and finisher of our faith"* (Hebrews 12:2A). Like that fencepost on the other side of the field, God and His Word are the landmarks that must not be removed.

Today, many think that they are unaffected by that which is around them and become careless with their attention. The devil knows that your focus affects your footsteps and so his goal is to get you to simply look somewhere else for just a moment. It is interesting to note what Jesus said in Luke 9:62, *"No man, having put his hand to the plough, and looking back, is fit for the kingdom of God."* Notice it doesn't say, "No man having put his hand to the plough and *going* back….All it takes for our furrow to become crooked is a "look."

We laugh at the little verse in Luke 17:32 and joke about having it memorized. But what a powerful truth is taught in just three words! *"Remember Lot's wife."* What is there to remember about this insignificant person? She *looked* back. She didn't *go* back—she never had that chance. She simply looked and was turned to a pillar of salt. You see, that's all the devil wants us to do because if he can get us to look—he knows our feet will eventually follow. I think of the people in the Bible who were destroyed, by a look.

> *And when the woman **saw** that the tree was good for food, and that it was pleasant to the **eyes**, and a tree to be desired to make one wise, she took of the fruit thereof, and did eat, and gave also unto her husband with her; and he did eat.—*Genesis 3:6

> *And Achan answered Joshua, and said, Indeed I have sinned against the* Lord *God of Israel, and thus and thus have I done: When I **saw** among the spoils a goodly Babylonish garment, and two hundred shekels of silver, and a wedge of gold of fifty shekels weight, then I coveted them, and took them; and, behold, they are hid in the earth in the midst of my tent, and the silver under it.* —Joshua 7:20–21

> *And Samson went down to Timnath, and **saw** a woman in Timnath of the daughters of the Philistines. And he came up, and told his father and his mother, and said, I have **seen** a woman in Timnath of the daughters of the Philistines: now therefore get her for me to wife.* —Judges 14:1–2

*And it came to pass in an eveningtide, that David arose from off his bed, and walked upon the roof of the king's house: and from the roof he **saw** a woman washing herself; and the woman was very beautiful to **look** upon.*—2 SAMUEL 11:2

Eve, Achan, Samson, and David. In each case it started with a look which led to a lust and finally to a leap. A big leap away from God! Where is your focus? Have you spent some time with God today? Are you reading His Word? Do you ever talk to Him? Do you let Him speak to you? An older gentleman and his wife were driving their car down the street. A car passed them with a young couple inside. The pretty young girl was sitting really close to the guy with her head on his shoulder. The older lady looked at her husband as they passed and said, "Remember, when we used to sit that close together?" The old man said, "I haven't moved."

A GRADUAL ACCEPTANCE

Words or phrases can be very subliminal and affect the way we think. We often say, "The fundamental Baptist movement…." Unfortunately, the word *movement* often describes our ranks. I can't think of any place in the Bible where we are described as a movement. But let me call your attention to Ephesians 6:10–14, where God calls us to **stand**! *"Finally, my brethren, be strong in the Lord, and in the power of his might. Put on the whole armour of God, that ye may be able to **stand** against the wiles of the devil. For we wrestle not against flesh and blood, but against principalities, against powers, against the rulers of the darkness of* *this world, against spiritual wickedness in high places. Wherefore take unto you the whole armour of God, that ye may be able to with**stand** in the evil day, and having done all to **stand**. **Stand** therefore, having your loins girt about with truth, and having on the breastplate of righteousness."* The command to stand indicates an unmovable position.

Movements can be very gradual and to the undiscerning eye even undetectable. If you looked at a full moon at ten o'clock at night it might not be very high in the sky. It would perhaps be positioned over on the eastern horizon. You could keep your eyes on the moon all night and probably never see it move, but by four in the morning, it would somehow be over in the western sky. I am told that Billy Graham in his early days was a powerful preacher who uncompromisingly preached the Word of God. In an early crusade in Los Angeles, over 4,000 people trusted Christ. The hand of God was upon him and leaders asked him to stay on and continue to preach. He didn't have any more sermons, but stood and for the next several nights read famous sermons from books. Many more were saved as a result.

Perhaps it was the success of those meetings that tempted Dr. Graham to become very pragmatic in his approach. His motive was to see more people saved, but his methods were now unbiblical. He began to partner with denominational leaders who rejected major doctrines of Scripture. Dr. Cedarholm shared with me that he sat on an airplane one day with Billy Graham and begged him to come back to the fundamental position he once held. Dr. Graham was cordial and thanked Dr. Cedarholm for the counsel, but said: "I have made up my mind. I want to see people saved no matter what I have to do to see that it happens." My friend, we must not compromise doctrine for the sake of results!

I recall vividly the day in chapel when Dr. Cedarholm announced that Dr. Jack Van Impe was someone to be careful about, and we were warned that he was on a road to compromise. I watched as students laughed at the "old man" in the pulpit and labeled it jealousy. Some students walked out of the chapel and left the school because they didn't feel it appropriate to criticize another "man of God." Now decades later, the proof's in the pudding, as they say. Dr. Van Impe often speaks favorably of the Church of Rome on his telecasts.

A GRIEVOUS AFFILIATION

Now as an "old man" myself, I've watched these changes over the years from a distance. Men and ministries that I wasn't personally familiar with are not where they were when they started. I have studied to some extent Baptist history, church history, and the history of revivals. There is no question that the times have changed, but unfortunately the

WHAT YOU DO WITH TRUTH WILL DETERMINE WHAT YOU DO WITH ERROR.

testimonies of many great ministries have also changed. But I never thought it would happen to anyone I knew and I was most certainly confident it wouldn't happen to me!

I had a very good friend in college with whom I spent a great deal of time. He and I played football together, sat in classes together (without him I would have never made it through English or Greek), went on ministry extension together, and quite frankly were just plain great friends. As we went soulwinning together and served in ministries, we often talked about our future in the Lord's work and all that God had put in our hearts to accomplish. He was in my wedding after graduation, and we stayed in touch even though God's will led us in different directions geographically.

One day, my friend called and informed me that he had taken a church and was now a senior pastor. I was thrilled for him and was confident that he would do a terrific job. I had heard him preach and because he was a tremendous student of the Bible, he was well prepared through his training and experience to now lead a flock. Better yet, he asked me as an evangelist to come and preach a revival meeting in his church. I was thrilled and eagerly anticipated the fellowship that we would enjoy as we put our hands on the same plow for a week.

Upon arrival at his church, we immediately sensed the same heart for ministry that we had always had, but something was definitely different. As I stood to preach, I knew in my heart that his congregation had been led in a different direction than where I stood. While I didn't understand all of the reasons why, I knew that my friend and I would not be able to partner together for that week of meetings like we had done in the past. *"Can two walk together, except they be agreed?"* (Amos 3:3). To be honest, we still enjoyed our time together and over these years have remained friends. But at the end of the week I said to him: "I don't think I can come back and preach another meeting for you." He replied: "And, I don't think that I will ever ask you."

While I have never attended the church he now pastors, I know that two decades ago, he instituted a contemporary service along with his traditional service on Sunday mornings.

Quite frankly, if he walked into my house today and had a need, I would do everything in my power to try to help. I love him and thank God for his influence in my life, but I can't lay aside clear biblical truth in order to partner with him for the sake of evangelism or for any other proper motive.

Churches and schools where I once preached have now suddenly taken *Baptist* out of their name. Men that I once preached for and with are now reading Scripture from Bibles I don't recognize. In other places, drum sets and electric guitars have replaced the piano and church organ. A young father told me that he sent his son to a Christian college recently, and his son related how one of his professors in class said to the students, "Now don't get sidetracked with the Great Commission!" The internet is filled with chitchat, tweets, and blogs criticizing what we used to stand for and defend in our pulpits.

When I came to West Coast Baptist College, one of my hopes was that we could eventually start an athletic program. Sports had been a huge part of my life, and my coaches were a great influence. After a few years, we started men's basketball, and I enjoyed watching our young men compete. Our team was scheduled to play in Phoenix at Southwestern Baptist College (they have since removed the word Baptist), and I decided to make the trip. Southwestern was a part of the Conservative Baptist Association. As I drove on to the campus and made my way to the gym, I thought about how Dr. Cedarholm for over twenty years of his ministry of evangelism had planted and preached in churches of the CBA. My mind raced to all of those stories he told us in preacher boys' class about his travels and the joy of seeing souls saved and churches established.

At halftime of the game, a curtain on the stage was pulled back and a band called "*In Snyc*" began to perform. As the drums were pounded and the guitars wined, I thought to myself: "Dr. Cedarholm gave his life and strength for this?" To be honest, I don't remember the score of that game or even whether we won or lost. I do remember driving away determined to dig my heels in a little deeper and straighten my back a little taller.

A FOCUSED PRIORITY

Later, we will look closely at the Apostle Paul's words in 2 Timothy 3. Whether or not you will be standing for truth a generation from now will be determined by what you do with the last two verses of that chapter. It all boils down to how you think, and Scripture must control your thinking if you will stay true to the One who gave us that Scripture. What you do with Truth will determine what you do with error. Paul reminds Timothy that *"All scripture is given by inspiration of God, and is profitable for doctrine, for reproof, for correction, for instruction in righteousness. That the man of God may be perfect, throughly furnished unto all good works"* (2 Timothy 3:16).

A TRUTH THAT STANDS THE TESTS

It is God's Word that is profitable for doctrine—that's what's right. It is profitable for reproof—that's what's wrong. It is profitable for correction—that's how to get right. And it is profitable for instruction in righteousness—that's how to stay right. I don't want to be wrong; I want to be right. If I am wrong, I want to know how to get right. And if I am right, I would like to know how to stay right! For that to happen, I must stay close to Scripture and let it guide my thinking exclusively. Remember the children of Issachar that we mentioned earlier? It says in 1 Chronicles 12:32 that they had *"an understanding of the times."* It adds in the next phrase, *"to know what Israel ought to do."* Where does one get the wisdom to know what to do when the times around us are changing? Paul told Timothy, *"Study to shew thyself approved unto God, a workman that needeth not to be ashamed, rightly dividing the word of truth"* (2 Timothy 2:15).

A THINKING THAT STANDS THE TEMPTATIONS

Is the Word of God the light and lamp for your feet? There are many distractions that will take your direction away from Truth very quickly. God is not looking for blenders but rather defenders of His inspired, inerrant, infallible, and preserved Word. To do that, we are going to have to think differently. We don't have to change. If we succumb to the thought that nothing lasts, that every ministry is altered with time, and that no one believes what our forefathers did, then we are doomed to failure.

If you are looking for your life and ministry to be called a success by God at the Judgment Seat of Christ, then Joshua 1:8 must be branded on your brain and fastened to every fiber of your life: *"This book of the law shall not depart out of thy mouth; but thou shalt meditate therein day and night, that thou mayest observe to do according to all that is written therein: for then thou shalt make thy way prosperous, and then thou shalt have good success."*

If we "think" that everything has to compromise at some point, then no doubt it will happen. Let's change our thinking! God doesn't change; the Bible doesn't change; and there is no reason for us to change.

TWO

THE TESTIMONY
TRUTH WILL KEEP US ON TRACK

*To the law and to the testimony: if they speak
not according to this word, it is because there is
no light in them.*—ISAIAH 8:20

I served a summer internship between my sophomore and junior year of college at the Woodcrest Baptist Church in Minneapolis, Minnesota with Dr. Clarke Poorman. He was a wonderful pastor and a great mentor in my life. I was young, immature, and in many ways directionless in my life at that time. He took a chance on me, and I am eternally grateful that he did. (It was during that summer that God called me to preach.)

One week, Pastor Poorman came to me and said, "John, the Sunday school teacher for the teens is going to be gone this week and I would like you to preach to the young people." I was speechless! I hadn't taken homiletics and I had never preached before except in a nursing home, which is a story for another book! He told me that he would be praying for me and was confident that I could do the job. That wasn't much of a comfort, but I went to work on a sermon. I decided to preach on Judas Iscariot. I called the message "Thirty Pieces of Silver."

I honestly did my best, but my best was about the worst anybody had ever done. I think I would have been fine except that the pastor had his wife sit in on the class. I was horrified. Her husband was an outstanding preacher—one of the best I had ever heard in my life—and I knew that I was in trouble. When it was over and the kids filed out, she waited for me at the back of the room. Mrs. Poorman was a very kind lady, but had a way of being very direct and frank. She said, "John, that was good." I thanked her and said, "Praise the Lord," but hardly believed her. I said, "Mrs. Poorman, I don't know where your husband gets all of his sermons." I was exhausted from the process of preparation and delivery and wondered if I could ever do it again. I will never forget what she did and what she said. She smiled and holding out her Bible in front of her said, "They're all in here," and walked away.

She was right! If you're looking for Truth there is only one place to search. Jesus prayed in John 17:17, *"Sanctify them through thy truth: thy word is truth."* Do you believe that everything you need for life and ministry is exclusively found in God's Word? The psalmist sure did. *"The law of the Lord is perfect, converting the soul: the testimony of the Lord is sure, making wise the simple. The statutes of the Lord are right, rejoicing the heart: the commandment of the Lord is pure, enlightening the eyes. The fear of the Lord is clean, enduring for ever: the judgments of the Lord are true and righteous altogether. More to be desired are they than gold, yea, than much fine gold: sweeter also than honey and the honeycomb. Moreover by them is thy servant warned: and in keeping of them there is great reward*" (Psalm 19:7–11).

I was sitting on the ordination counsel for one of our graduates. For over three hours, several of us examined his doctrine and asked him questions about his life and ministry. He did a great job and said nothing that would have caused any great alarm. When we finished, one of the veteran pastors looked at him and said: "You've done a great job, and I appreciate your presentation of your beliefs and the way you have answered our questions. But I want you to go home and do something for me. As you have answered our questions, you have often started by saying, 'I believe, or I think'. I want you to stand in front of a mirror and every day practice saying: 'The Bible says.' I have been a pastor in this city for a quarter of a century and found that people in this town do not care what I think or believe, but they will listen if I tell them what the Bible says."

What awesome advice! *"To the law and to the testimony: if they speak not according to this word, it is because there is no light in them*" (Isaiah 8:20). Let's take a close look at the *testimony* that God has given us to study, to stand upon, and proclaim.

THE PENNING OF THE WORD
THE DIVINE AUTHOR WAS GOD

The Bible is not a collection of mere stories about man or advice from man. The Bible is God's Book. It is called the "Holy Bible" because it was written by a holy God—the One and only God. How can we argue with what the Bible says about itself in 2 Peter 1:20–21? *"Knowing this first, that no prophecy of the scripture is of any private interpretation. For the prophecy came not in old time by the will of man: but holy men of God spake as they were moved by the Holy Ghost."* God breathed His very words into the heart of the human authors to be written and preserved for all of eternity. *"All scripture is given by inspiration of God"* (2 Timothy 3:16A) means every word is a word from God.

We don't like our words being twisted or misinterpreted. We get offended when someone misquotes us or adds their interpretation to what we said. God wrote the Bible and put his own copyright on its content. *"Ye shall not add unto the word which I command you, neither shall ye diminish ought from it, that ye may keep the commandments of the Lord your God which I command you"* (Deuteronomy 4:2). *"What thing soever I command you, observe to do it: thou shalt not add thereto, nor diminish from it"* (Deuteronomy 12:32). *"Add thou not unto his words, lest he reprove thee, and thou be found a liar"* (Proverbs 30:6). *"And if any man shall take away from the words of the book of this prophecy, God shall take away his part out of the book of life, and out of the holy city, and from the things which are written in this book"* (Revelation 22:19).

THE HUMAN AUTHORS WERE GUIDED

"As they were moved by the Holy Ghost," Peter tells us in 2 Peter 1:21B. While 2 Timothy 3:16 says that *"All scripture is given by inspiration of God,"* there are several places in the Bible where God reminds us of how this was explicitly done. *"Take thee a roll of a book, and write therein all the words that I have spoken unto thee against Israel, and against Judah, and against all the*

nations, from the day I spake unto thee, from the days of Josiah, even unto this day" (Jeremiah 36:2). *"The word of the Lord came expressly unto Ezekiel the priest, the son of Buzi, in the land of the Chaldeans by the river Chebar; and the hand of the* LORD *was there upon him"* (Ezekiel 1:3). *"Men and brethren, this scripture must needs have been fulfilled, which the Holy Ghost by the mouth of David spake before concerning Judas, which was guide to them that took Jesus"* (Acts 1:16). *"And I heard a voice from heaven saying unto me, Write, Blessed are the dead which die in the Lord from henceforth: Yea, saith the Spirit, that they may rest from their labours; and their works do follow them"* (Revelation 14:13).

How big is your God? Is your God big enough to create the entire universe in six days by speaking it into existence? Is your God big enough to save your soul from a literal lake of fire and give you eternal life in heaven? If by faith you believe in that God, then why do you doubt that the same God could not guide the human authors to pen His exact words and preserve them for us today? A little God exhumes big questions, but a big God eliminates all questions.

A LITTLE GOD EXHUMES BIG QUESTIONS, BUT A BIG GOD ELIMINATES ALL QUESTIONS.

Remember, where you will be standing a generation from now will be determined by what you do with Scripture. Building your life and ministry on the "rock" of God's Truth will enable you to be standing when others have been washed away by the storms of life because their foundation was sand. *"Therefore whosoever heareth these sayings of mine, and doeth them, I will liken him unto a wise man, which built his house upon a rock: And the rain descended, and the floods came, and the winds blew, and beat upon that house; and it fell not: for it was founded upon a rock. And everyone that heareth these sayings of mine, and doeth them not, shall be likened unto a foolish man, which built his house upon the sand: And the rain descended, and the floods came, and the winds blew, and beat upon that house; and it fell: and great was the fall of it*" (Matthew 7:24–27).

Standing or falling will be determined by what you build upon. Much is being taught and much is written, and you can choose to follow whoever and whatever you will. The wise man will believe and build on that which is penned by God.

THE PROCLAMATION OF THE WORD
PROCLAIMED IN THE MINISTRY

God's Word is to be proclaimed in the ministry. Plagiarism is a serious offense in education and is dealt with severely by an instructor. Explicit copyrights prohibit us from stealing someone else's work. God doesn't mind—in fact He demands—that we "plagiarize" His Word. "*Preach the word*" Paul plainly tells Timothy in 2 Timothy 4:2A. He doesn't advise us to preach "about" the Word, or "around" the Word, but the absolute Word. In Acts 5:20 the apostles were admonished by an angel to "*Go, stand and speak in the temple to the people all the words of this life.*"

God might bless my homiletic outline; He might bless my stories and illustrations; He might bless my style of delivery; but He doesn't promise to do so. He promises to bless His Word! "*For as the rain cometh down, and the snow from heaven,* and returneth not thither, but watereth the earth, and maketh it bring forth and bud, that it may give seed to the sower, and bread to the eater: So shall my word be that goeth forth out of my mouth: it shall not return unto me void, but it shall accomplish that which I please, and it shall prosper in the thing whereto I sent it" (Isaiah 55:10–11).

God took great care in giving us His Word as we have already seen. Someone carefully and faithfully communicated it to you. Now you have that awesome privilege and responsibility to handle it and deliver it with the same carefulness. Ponder carefully the following admonition: *"Bow down thine ear, and hear the words of the wise, and apply thine heart unto my knowledge. For it is a pleasant thing if thou keep them within thee; they shall withal be fitted in thy lips. That thy trust may be in the LORD, I have made known to thee this day, even to thee. Have not I written to thee excellent things in counsels and knowledge, That I might make thee know the certainty of the words of truth; that thou mightest answer the words of truth to them that send unto thee?"* (Proverbs 22:17–21).

> TALK IS IMPORTANT TO BE SURE, BUT IT IS OUR WALK THAT MAKES OUR TALK WALK.

PRACTICED IN THE MILIEU

God's Word is to be practiced in the milieu. Your milieu is your day-to-day environment and lifestyle. Quite honestly, proclaiming God's Word is the easy part—practicing it in your everyday life is much more difficult. But no one really cares for what we preach if they can't see it in our practice. I love how God instructs us to weave the Scripture into the milieu of our lives, particularly in the context of our families, in Deuteronomy 6:6–9: *"And these words, which I command thee this day, shall be in thine heart: And thou shalt teach them diligently unto thy children, and shalt talk of them when thou sittest in thine house, and when thou walkest by the way, and when thou liest down, and when thou risest up. And thou shalt bind them for a sign upon thine hand, and they shall be as frontlets between thine eyes. And thou shalt write them upon the posts of thy house, and on thy gates."*

While our talk is important, it is our walk that makes our talk walk! Talk is cheap, but walk is expensive. Early in his life, the apostle Peter could talk a good game, but his walk fell woefully short. By the end of his life, his walk matched his words as he courageously yielded to martyrdom for what he believed and preached.

I am convinced that there are skeptics who have studied more diligently the Word of God than I have. They have done so in an effort to find errors or contradiction. Simply knowing the Word of God is not enough—we must endeavor to live what we know. Jesus said in John 13:17: *"If ye know these things, happy are ye if ye do them."* James adds in chapter 1:22–25: *"But be ye doers of the word, and not hearers only, deceiving your own selves. For if any be a hearer of the word, and not a doer, he is like unto a man beholding his natural face in a glass: For he beholdeth himself, and goeth his way, and straightway forgetteth what manner of man he was. But whoso looketh into the perfect law of liberty, and continueth therein, he being not a forgetful hearer, but a doer of the work, this man shall be blessed in his deed."*

The Apostle Paul didn't want to preach the Truth and then destroy that Truth by the way he lived. He told the Corinthian church, *"But I keep under my body, and bring it into subjection: lest that by any means, when I have preached to others, I myself should be a castaway"* (1 Corinthians (9:27). Are we concerned today that our practice matches our proclamation? In Acts 17, Paul's manner and his message had an impact. In verse 2 it says, *"And Paul, as his manner was, went in unto them, and three sabbath days reasoned with them out of the scriptures."* Paul didn't change his methods or manners to try to blend in with the culture of Thessalonica. He practiced and preached the Scriptures consistently. In verse 6 of the same chapter, the Jews said: *"These that have turned the world upside down are come hither also."*

The world today needs to be turned upside down, or maybe right side up, but this cannot happen until we in our lives and ministries proclaim and practice the Word of God.

THE PROMISE OF THE WORD
GOD'S WORD IS TRUE

Why do we question God? Why do we doubt His authenticity? *"God is not a man, that he should lie; neither the son of man, that he should repent: hath he said, and shall he not do it? or hath he spoken, and shall he not make it good?"* (Numbers 23:19). Again, God's Word speaks for itself: *"Blessed be the LORD, that hath given rest unto his people Israel, according to all that he promised; there hath not failed one word of all his good promise, which he promised by the hand of Moses his servant"* (1 Kings 8:56). *"The works of his hands are verity and judgment; all his commandments are sure"* (Psalm 111:7). *"For I am the LORD: I will speak, and the word that I shall speak shall come to pass"* (Ezekiel 12:25A).

I know for the skeptic it is unreasonable and even ridiculous to defend the Word with the Word, but I love Hebrews 6:13: *"For when God made promise to Abraham, because he could swear by no greater, he sware by himself."* God said, "Abraham—I would love to give you a confirmation that what I am promising to you will come to pass, but there is no greater confirmation than me—so you'll just have to take my word for it!" He goes on to say, *"For men verily swear by the greater: and an oath for confirmation is to them an end of all strife. Wherein God, willing more abundantly to shew unto the heirs of promise the immutability of his counsel, confirmed it by an oath: That by two immutable things, in which it was impossible for God to lie, we might have a strong consolation, who have fled for refuge to lay hold upon the hope set before us"* (Hebrews 6:16–18). Is there anyone greater than God? Who are you going to trust? God says it is impossible for Him to lie. You can believe or deny that truth, but your obstinate will won't change God's omniscient will.

God's Word is true and will be the final authority and judge of our life and ministry. *"He that rejecteth me, and receiveth not my words, hath one that judgeth him: the word that I have spoken, the same shall judge him in the last day"* (John 12:48). Take the chance if you want to see if you are smarter than God, but you are a big loser if you're wrong.

GOD'S WORD IS TESTED

God's Word withstands every test man can give it because God made sure that it was tested. *"The words of the LORD are pure* words: as silver tried in a furnace of earth, purified seven times. Thou shalt keep them, O LORD, thou shalt preserve them from this generation for ever" (Psalm 12:6–7). Psalm 18:30 says: *"As for God, his way is perfect: the word of the LORD is tried: he is a buckler to all those that trust in him."* If God tested His Word before He gave it to us, why do we constantly try to tweak it? We can't improve on perfection!

One of my sons was preaching in a little country town in the hills of North Carolina. I happened to be in the area and had a free night so I went to hear him. I met the pastor before the service and we enjoyed some good fellowship. He was a young man in his thirties and just a few years into the ministry. He told me how he had gone to a little Bible college in the hills and while there fell in love with the New International Version of the Bible. He said, "I could understand it and it was easy to memorize and preach and so I did."

After he took the church, his grandfather, who was an old time evangelist, came to hear him one night. The old gentleman listened carefully to his grandson as he preached from that NIV Bible. No one responded at the invitation. He had been preaching for three years in that church and no one had ever walked the aisle to be saved. After the service, his elderly grandfather took him aside and said: "Son, you really like that NIV Bible don't you?" The young preacher said that he did and began to explain how much he enjoyed studying in it and preaching from it. The old man said, "I would like you to do me a favor. I want you to take the next month and study from your old King James Bible and preach from it for the next four Sundays. Will you promise me that you will?" The pastor told me that he deeply respected his grandfather and promised him that he would.

He said, "Brother Goetsch, I had my devotions in that King James Bible, studied from it, and prepared my Sunday message from it that next week. I walked into the pulpit and preached from it the next Sunday and when I gave the invitation a man came forward trusting Christ as his Saviour. Ever since that day, I have used the KJV and we haven't had a Sunday since where someone did not get saved!" He said, "I don't know much about the issue of the versions but I know that this old book is tried and tested." Now you could label me a pragmatist if that was my only argument for using the King James Bible, but I will tell you that you don't have to be a rocket scientist to figure out that God blesses His tried and tested Word. We don't need to be tampering, tearing down, or touching up the old Book. God's Word is tested.

GOD'S WORD IS TIMELESS

Man's life is frail and his strength is fleeting, but God's Word will not fail. *"The voice said, Cry. And he said, What shall I cry? All flesh is grass, and all the goodliness thereof is as the flower of the field. The grass withereth, the flower fadeth: because the spirit of the LORD bloweth upon it: surely the people is grass. The grass withereth, the flower fadeth: but the word of our God shall stand for ever"* (Isaiah 40:6–8). Jesus states in Mark 13:31, *"Heaven and earth shall pass away: but my words shall not pass away."* The psalmist makes it clear in Psalm 119:89 when he states, *"For ever O LORD, thy word is settled in heaven."*

The chorus of an old hymn puts it plainly: "The Bible stands tho' the hills may tumble; it will firmly stand when the earth shall crumble; I will plant my feet on its firm foundation for the Bible stands." We need to heed the words of the stanza that says, "The Bible stands every test we give it, for its Author is Divine. By grace alone I expect to live it and to prove it and make it mine." You might outlast your money; you might outlast your church; you might outlast your government; but you will never outlast your Bible—it is eternal! *"Concerning thy testimonies, I have known of old that thou hast founded them for ever"* (Psalm 119:152).

GOD'S WORD IS TRIUMPHANT

God's Word changes hearts and lives. *"Wherefore thus saith the LORD God of hosts, Because ye speak this word, behold, I will make my words in thy mouth fire, and this people wood, and it shall devour them"* (Jeremiah 5:14). I love the words of that same prophet Jeremiah in chapter 23:28–29: *"The prophet that hath a dream, let him tell a dream; and he that hath my word, let him speak my word faithfully. What is the chaff to the wheat? saith the LORD. Is not my word like as a fire? saith the LORD; and like a hammer that breaketh the rock in pieces?"* This old world is pretty hard and some people's hearts are like a rock, but there is a Book that can break them to pieces! Man doesn't even know his own heart or what he needs. Our hearts are deceitful and wicked but there is a Book that can uncover the need in any heart and meet that need. *"For the word of God is quick, and powerful, and sharper than any twoedged sword, piercing even to the dividing asunder of soul and spirit, and of the joints and marrow, and is a discerner of the thoughts and intents of the heart"* (Hebrews 4:12).

THE POWER OF THE WORD

I have already touched on this, but I can't close this chapter without rejoicing in the power of God's Word! It is the weapon that God has given to us to accomplish His work in this world. *"And take the helmet of salvation, and the sword of the Spirit, which is the word of God"* (Ephesians 6:17). I don't know about you but I want my hand to be on the weapon that the Spirit of God uses. *"It is the spirit that quickeneth; the flesh profiteth nothing: the words that I speak unto you, they are spirit, and they are life"* (John 6:63).

THE WORD OF GOD HAS POWER TO CONVICT

God uses some powerful metaphors to describe the ability of His Word. He calls it a hammer, a fire, and a sword. It can do what no human method or machine can accomplish. It cuts through all the resistance and gets to the heart. Saul of Tarsus was about as hard a man to the Truth as they come. He was convinced he was right and was putting to death those that disagreed with him. But when he heard God's words, he melted like a block of ice in a furnace. *"And Saul, yet breathing out threatenings and slaughter against the disciples of the Lord, went unto the high priest, And desired of him letters to Damascus to the synagogues, that if he found any of this way, whether they were men or women, he might bring them bound unto Jerusalem. And as he journeyed, he came near Damascus: and suddenly there shined round about him a light from heaven: And he fell to the earth, and heard a voice saying unto him, Saul, Saul, why persecutest thou me? And he said, Who art thou, Lord? And the Lord said, I am Jesus whom thou persecutest: it is hard for thee to kick against the pricks. And he trembling and astonished said, Lord, what wilt thou have me to do?"* (Acts 9:1–6A).

In the summer of 1967, I sat in a teen camp in northern Wisconsin. I was a Baptist and president of the youth group at my church. My dad was the chairmen of the deacons in that church and my mom was a Sunday school teacher. My sister was the church pianist. I was a good kid by most people's standards but in God's sight I was lost. That first night of camp, Dr. Eric Folsom from St. Petersburg, Florida stood and preached on the subject of Hell from Luke 16. As I listened, the still small voice of God convicted me and said, "John, that's the place that you will spend eternity in unless you trust Christ as your personal Saviour." I knew the Holy Spirit was right. I had no assurance of eternal life, but when the invitation started, my stubborn German pride kicked in, and I resisted the Holy Spirit's voice. But God's Word continued to burn in my heart throughout that night and all the next day.

The next night, August 1, 1967, I couldn't bear up under that conviction any longer. I walked down the aisle with a preacher who was sitting behind me by the name of Don Pfaffe. He led me to a side room, took me through the Roman's Road and I gladly trusted Christ as my Saviour. That powerful conviction turned to a powerful assurance in an instant, as by faith I came to Christ. I have seen the Word of God convict hundreds over these years. Thank God that His Word has power to convict!

THE WORD OF GOD HAS POWER TO CONVERT

It is the Word of God that brings about salvation. *"So then faith cometh by hearing, and hearing by the word of God"* (Romans 10:17). James 1:21 exhorts, *"Wherefore lay apart all filthiness and superfluity of naughtiness, and receive with meekness the engrafted word, which is able to save your souls."* The psalmist puts it simply, *"The law of the LORD is perfect, converting the soul"* (Psalm 19:7A).

The Apostle Paul was a gifted man and trained in the finest of schools. But following his conversion, he realized quickly that it was not his ability or eloquence that would produce fruit. He understood clearly where the power was for preaching. That power was not in his words, but God's! *"And I, brethren, when I came to you, came not with excellency of speech or of wisdom, declaring unto you the testimony of God. For I determined not to know any thing among you, save Jesus Christ, and him crucified. And I was with you in weakness, and in fear, and in much trembling. And my speech and my preaching was not with enticing words of man's wisdom, but in demonstration of the Spirit and of power: That your faith should not stand in the wisdom of men, but in the power of God"* (1 Corinthians 2:1–5).

THE WORD OF GOD HAS POWER TO CLEANSE

Years ago, I was soulwinning with a pastor in the Detroit, Michigan area. We were in a poor neighborhood and had been invited into a house that was very dirty, to say the least. As we were walking down the sidewalk after our visit, the pastor shook his body all over like a dog coming out of a lake and said, "I feel like I need to go home and take a bath!"

We often feel that way spiritually in this old wicked world. The prophet Micah reminds us of the pollution of this world. *"Arise ye, and depart; for this is not your rest: because it is polluted, it shall destroy you, even with a sore destruction"* (Micah 2:10). God invites us to take a bath in His Word each day: *"Now ye are clean through the word which I have spoken unto you"* (John 15:3). Peter writes: *"Whereby are given unto us exceeding great and precious promises: that by these ye might be partakers of the divine nature, having escaped the corruption that is in the world through lust"* (2 Peter 1:4). God's desire for our heart is *"That he might sanctify and cleanse it with the washing of water by the word"* (Ephesians 5:26).

Have you let God take you to the cleaners lately? There is no way for us to stay pure in a polluted world without the power of His Word.

THE WORD OF GOD HAS POWER TO CONSTRUCT

Paul writes in Acts 20:32: *"And now, brethren, I commend you to God, and to the word of his grace, which is able to build you up, and to give you an inheritance among all them which are sanctified."* Without proper nourishment, the body cannot grow. The same is true of the soul. God commands us to eat. *"As newborn babes, desire the sincere milk of the word, that ye may grow thereby"* (1 Peter 2:2). While we start with milk, we must eventually get to the meat if we want to mature. *"For every one that useth milk is unskilful in the word of righteousness: for he is a babe. But strong meat belongeth to them that are of full age, even those who by reason of use have their senses exercised to discern both good and evil"* (Hebrews 5:13–14).

Spiritual maturity doesn't happen overnight. God carefully constructs our lives step by step so that we will not crumble under pressure. *"Whom shall he teach knowledge? and whom shall he make to understand doctrine? them that are weaned from the milk, and drawn from the breasts. For precept must be upon precept, precept upon precept; line upon line, line upon line; here a little, and there a little"* (Isaiah 28:9–10). Every day we can become stronger in our walk with God because His Word has power to construct.

> THIS BOOK WILL KEEP YOU FROM SIN OR SIN WILL KEEP YOU FROM THIS BOOK.

THE WORD OF GOD HAS POWER TO COUNSEL

"The entrance of thy words giveth light; it giveth understanding unto the simple" (Psalm 119:130). When we are in a quandary, not knowing which way to go, we should pray the prayer of the psalmist in Psalm 119:133, *"Order my steps in thy word: and let not any iniquity have dominion over me."*

God gives us good advice through Solomon of old as he writes to his son: *"My son, keep thy father's commandment, and forsake not the law of thy mother: Bind them continually upon thine heart, and tie them about thy neck. When thou goest, it shall lead thee; when thou sleepest, it shall keep thee; and when thou awakest, it shall talk with thee. For the commandment is a lamp;*

and the law is light; and reproofs of instruction are the way of life" (Proverbs 6:20–23).

I remember vividly one day God convicting me about confronting someone about an issue. I didn't want to do so because he was older than I was and in a position of great authority. I argued with the Lord and gave Him all the reasons why I didn't want to do as He prompted me. I put the issue off and decided that He could deal with the person without my help. The next morning I picked up my Bible for my devotions. It was the 24th day of the month, and I was in the habit of reading the chapter in Proverbs that aligned with the day. I got to verse 10, and God counseled me: *"If thou faint in the day of adversity, thy strength is small."* I went to the phone and called the brother. We had a sweet time of resolving the matter. How I thank the Lord for His Word that counsels.

THE WORD OF GOD HAS POWER TO COMFORT

We may not need comfort every day, but there will be days when we will need little else. The psalmist cried, *"Mine eyes fail for thy word, saying, When wilt thou comfort me?"* (Psalm 119:82). The prophet Jeremiah had a tough life and a rough ministry, but he found comfort in God's Word. *"Thy words were found, and I did eat them; and thy word was unto me the joy and rejoicing of mine heart: for I am called by thy name, O LORD God of hosts"* (Jeremiah 15:16).

A man that greatly influenced my life was Dr. Richard Weeks. He used to come to my football games when I was in high school and sit up in the stands and pray that God would get a hold of my life. When I surrendered to God and went to Bible college, he became one of my favorite teachers and a wonderful mentor for ministry.

Not long after I graduated, his wife died and soon after Dr. Weeks suffered a stroke. Over the next several years the doctors said that he suffered from hundreds of strokes and each time they would take away a little more of his memory and his physical strength. I enjoyed going by and visiting him as often as I could, and he was always a great encouragement to me.

One day my pastor phoned and informed me that Dr. Weeks had just a few days to live. He had stopped eating and drinking and it was simply a matter of time. He was in a hospital in Freeport, Illinois where his daughter Ruthie and her family lived. My pastor was in Wisconsin and I was holding a revival meeting in central Illinois. We decided that each of us would drive to Freeport, meet there, and go by and see Dr. Weeks one last time.

When we arrived at the hospital, Ruthie met us and as we went into the elevator she said: "Dad won't be able to say anything. In fact, he can't even blink his eyes in response, or squeeze your hand. But he will know that you are here, so just talk to him like normal." As we entered the room, Dr. Weeks was lying on his side in a fetal position. His eyes were glassy and he stared through the rail on his hospital bed. My pastor and I knelt down in front of him. Pastor said, "Dr. Weeks, it's Pastor. I wanted to come by and see you and I brought with me Bro. Goetsch." There was no response from his body or face. Those eyes stared straight ahead.

Pastor and I both made some additional small talk but it was difficult as both of us were at a loss for what to say. I will never forget as Pastor Lincoln pulled from his pocket his Bible and said: "Dr. Weeks, why don't I read some from your favorite passage of Scripture?" Without taking his eyes off of Dr. Weeks, he turned a few pages in his Bible and began to quote Psalm 23: *"The Lord is my shepherd; I shall not want. He maketh me to lie down...."* As he began verse 2, tears began to trickle from the sides of Dr. Week's eyes. He was hearing the Word of God that he loved and it was comforting him!

A few days later, Ruthie called and told me that her Dad had gone home and asked if I could come and read Scripture at his funeral. Dr. Weeks no longer needed the comfort from the Scripture that day, but I sure did! *"For whatsoever things were written aforetime were written for our learning, that we through patience and comfort of the scriptures might have hope"* (Romans 15:4).

God gave us the Testimony to keep us on track. The Bible is not some stuffy old book that no one can understand. It is living Truth that changes lives and guides us in every step of our pilgrim journey on earth. No doubt many a mother or father has written these words in the front of a child's Bible upon presentation: "This book will keep you from sin or sin will keep you from this book."

God gave us His Testimony so that we wouldn't stray from Truth. We need to read it, live it, and preach it. Without it we will be blown hither and yon with every wind of doctrine that comes along. *"And he gave some, apostles; and some, prophets; and some, evangelists; and some, pastors and teachers; For the perfecting of the saints, for the work of the ministry, for the edifying of the body of Christ: Till we all come in the unity of the faith, and of the knowledge of the Son of God, unto a perfect man, unto the measure of the stature of the fullness of Christ: That we henceforth be no more children, tossed to and fro, and carried about with every wind of doctrine, by the sleight of men, and cunning craftiness, whereby they lie in wait to deceive; But speaking the truth in love, may grow up into him in all things, which is the head, even Christ"* (Ephesians 4:11–15).

Stay with the Truth and you'll stay on track!

THREE

THE TRAGEDY
COMPROMISE IS NOT AN
EVENT—IT'S AN EVOLUTION

*Remove not the ancient landmark, which thy
fathers have set.*—PROVERBS 22:28

The story is told of a man who sold fish alongside of the road near his town. Sales were not too good, and it was a struggle to make ends meet financially. One day a man stopped by and asked how things were going. The man told the visitor that it was difficult, and he really didn't know what to do. The visitor advised him to make an attractive sign to advertise his table of fish. This would attract those who were passing by and otherwise might not have noticed.

The man thought this was a great idea, and so he went down to a sign maker and hired him to paint the sign. The proprietor asked the man what he wanted the sign to say. He thought on that for a moment and decided on this: "Fresh Fish For Sale Today." The sign was made, delivered, and within a few days towered above the passing crowds advertising the man's fish.

Not long after the sign was erected, a man stopped and said: "Hey, I like your sign, but you have too many words. You don't really need the word 'Fresh.' After all, you wouldn't sell anyone rotten fish, would you? Of course they're 'fresh;' you're an honest man and wouldn't sell anything else." He was right, the man thought, and so he took down the sign and with his handsaw sawed off the end of the board with the word "Fresh." Now his sign simply read: "Fish For Sale Today."

He had no more than hung the sign when a lady stopped and said, "Sir, you have a beautiful sign, but you have too many words. You really don't need the word 'Today.' Of course they are for sale today. They're not for sale tomorrow or yesterday. It is redundant to have the word 'today' on your sign." She was right. The man took the sign down and sawed off the other end of the board with the word "Today." Now his sign read: "Fish For Sale."

A short time later another passerby stopped and looked at the sign and said: "Nice sign—but you have too many words. You don't need the words 'For Sale.' Of course they are for sale. You aren't giving them away for free are you?" He too was right the man thought, and so he took down the sign once more and chopped off the words "For Sale." His sign now simply had one word "Fish."

No more than ten minutes passed when a rather angry man stopped at the Fish stand and yelled: "You don't need that stupid sign! We can smell your fish a mile away!" The man reached up and took the sign down.

Compromise is not an event—it's an evolution. We often have the notion that a person just falls over the cliff into sin one day or that a church one Sunday evening decides in a business meeting that it no longer believes in the Bible. We may hear about the compromise one day but it didn't happen in one day. The praise band with drums and electric guitars didn't just appear on the platform on a Sunday night in July. A church may cancel soulwinning or Sunday night services,

> COMPROMISE IS NOT AN EVENT— IT'S AN EVOLUTION.

but the thought process of doing so was gradual. The fact that present-day churches are hosting couple's retreats involving unmarried couples is not because of an oversight or because somebody forgot to check the registrations. The fact that a Bible college requires their students to read their assignments from a buffet of Bible versions doesn't take place because a professor was able to sneak in with a phony resumé. A denomination that allows women preachers or gay bishops doesn't just vote to do so at an annual meeting.

Compromise takes place gradually and is often difficult to detect until it's too late. If you take a frog and throw him into a kettle of boiling water, he will jump out of that kettle and hop away before you can blink. But if you take that frog and put him in a kettle of room temperature water, he will swim around and enjoy the bath. If you place that kettle on the stove and turn up the heat, that water will warm gradually until it boils. And do you know what? That frog will swim around in that boiling water until it cooks him to death!

It is my fear that a good number of God's people, churches, schools, and denominations are swimming around in dangerous waters. Their doctrinal beliefs and creeds are in good order. In some cases those haven't changed for decades, but they are oblivious to the gradual evolution that is taking place. The water is boiling and about to snatch their life, but because of pride, peer pressure, or politics, they are afraid to jump. What once was a dynamic life or ministry has now reached its expiration date. As they say, "everything has shelf-life" and the product has reached that point and must be cast away. Someone or something else will need to be raised up to take its place.

YOUR GREATEST STRENGTH CAN BECOME YOUR GREATEST WEAKNESS.

Well, let's see if we can buck this tragic trend. We're not frogs or mindless products on a shelf. God gave us a brain and it's about time we start using it to think biblically. Put your "saw" away. We don't have to start chopping off elements of Truth. In 2 Timothy 3, the Apostle Paul shows us several contributing components to compromise.

A SELFISH PRAGMATISM

Second Timothy 3:1–2 says, *"This know also, that in the last days perilous times shall come. For men shall be lovers of their own selves, covetous, boasters, proud, blasphemers, disobedient to parents, unthankful, unholy."* Your greatest strength can often become your greatest weakness. The devil loves to prey on the positives in our lives. He looks at what drives us or what we are passionate about and then uses it as a weapon against us.

For instance, someone may have what we would call a "big heart." They would help anyone who has a need. The Bible would call it a gift of "helps." God uses this kind of person greatly as they use their resources to encourage and strengthen others. But the devil will send someone along who isn't legitimate—in fact, he is an outright liar. But this big-hearted Christian with a desire to help buys his story hook, line, and sinker. He gets taken for a ride because his strength became his weakness.

The truth is that no godly person intends to backslide. No Bible believing church is planted with a goal to compromise. No Christian college or school was ever started with the goal of turning out apathetic or godless graduates. Rather, we want to do something great! We want to make an impact for Christ on this world with our life and ministry. We'd like to leave a footprint for God on this planet before we leave. I honestly don't think there are too many Christians who want to be rebuked at the Judgment Seat of Christ. Local churches don't set a goal to close their doors. Most people I know pray for revival and for souls to come to Christ.

The devil observes these desires, and while he may not change the goal, he works on changing the reason for the goal. Have you ever seen God use you to accomplish something that you prayed for only to forget when it happened to thank the Lord? As people began to praise and thank you, you gladly took that praise for yourself and began to think that if it hadn't been for you, it never would have happened. I'm not against using the term "soulwinner" but it can play right into this trap. We say: "That person is a great soulwinner." In reality, God is the One who wins the soul. We can only lead people to Him. People might say: "If you hadn't preached that sermon I would never have gotten saved." Well, God used you to preach the sermon, but again it's God that saves.

Our biggest enemy is self. D.L. Moody used to say, "The man I fear the most is the one who walks underneath this hat." When Abraham Lincoln was running for president of the United States, a reporter asked him, "Do you fear any of your opponents?" Lincoln thought for a brief moment and responded, "Yes, one." The reporter was surprised for Lincoln was doing very well in the campaign. He said, "Really! Which one do you fear?" Lincoln said: "A man named Lincoln. If I am defeated, I will be defeated by Lincoln." No doubt it was that humility that made Abraham Lincoln one of our greatest presidents.

Most of our downfall can be attributed to selfishness and when it comes to ministry, it is often a selfish pragmatism. We want to do something great, but soon we are willing to compromise anything in order to achieve that success. We don't like the thought of being a failure or not accomplishing all of our goals and dreams, and so we are willing to compromise biblical principles to achieve those goals.

It's not wrong to want to win people to Christ, sing a good special, memorize Scripture, build a bus route, write a book, or plant a church. But why do you want to do these things? Is it for God's glory or your own? God doesn't share His glory. *"I am the LORD: that is my name: and my glory will I not give to another, neither my praise to graven images"* (Isaiah 42:8). With God, the way up is down. *"And whosoever shall exalt himself shall be abased; and he that shall humble himself shall be exalted"* (Matthew 23:12). We were not created for our glory but for God's glory. *"Thou art worthy, O Lord, to receive glory and honour and power: for thou hast created all things, and for thy pleasure they are and were created"* (Revelation 4:11). You and I have one goal—to please God and bring glory to Him as a result.

We manifest our selfishness when we talk about *my* life, *my* church, *my* ministry, etc. Paul humbly writes in 2 Corinthians 4:5, *"For we preach not ourselves, but Christ Jesus the Lord; and ourselves your servants for Jesus' sake."* There is no greater model in the Bible of unselfishness than our Lord Jesus Christ Himself. Paul speaks of Him in his letter to the Philippians and encourages them to develop this unselfish thinking in their lives. *"Let nothing be done through strife or vainglory; but in lowliness of mind let each esteem other better than themselves. Look not every man on his own things, but every man also on the things of others. Let this mind be in you, which was also in Christ Jesus: Who, being in the form of God, thought it not robbery to be equal with God: But made himself of no reputation, and took upon him the form of a servant, and was made in the likeness of men: And being found in fashion as a man, he humbled himself, and became obedient unto death, even the death of the cross"* (Philippians 2:3–8).

GOD DOESN'T CALL MEN TO BUILD A CROWD. HE CALLS THEM TO BUILD A CHURCH.

When one studies modernism, liberalism, neo-orthodoxy, new-evangelicalism, the seeker sensitive movement, and the emergent church movement there is always the thinking that we have become too narrow minded, too straight-laced, too exclusive, or too divisive. We could grow so much faster and larger if we would loosen our standards, soften our message, and become less rigid in our beliefs. Soon growth rather than godliness becomes the goal, and it plays right into our selfish nature. Responding to a question about the music in his church, a pastor said: "I know it's wrong, but the church is growing." God didn't call you to build a crowd—He called you to build a church!

We want to do something great, but we must remember that our old sinful flesh is selfish in its makeup. That unbridled selfishness will cause us to become pragmatic in our approach to ministry in order to keep our ego satisfied.

Years ago I was scheduled to preach an anniversary Sunday for a church. We arrived on Saturday and the church property was a beehive of activity as they prepared for the big day. The church was several years old and the pastor told me that every year on their anniversary they had broken their previous attendance record. I think the highest attendance at that time was just over three hundred, which was quite impressive for the time that they had been in existence. The pastor told me they were shooting for four hundred the following day, and everything was in order to reach that mark.

That evening at the men's prayer meeting, I counted the chairs that were packed into the tiny auditorium. There were just over 80 chairs. Outside, they had built some make-shift benches for the children to sit on in a special service that my wife would conduct. There was room on those benches for eighty to one-hundred children. We spent some time in prayer, and I was anticipating a great day.

The next morning, the place was packed. Every chair in the auditorium was filled and another fifteen stood across the back. My wife's service was likewise full with close to one hundred children. I'm sure the nursery room had a full house as well and several of the workers were running hither and yon throughout the day carrying out their duties. It was an awesome day and several trusted Christ as Saviour.

At the end of the service, one of the ushers brought a small piece of paper to the pastor. Due to the cramped quarters, I was standing right next to him when he received it, and I saw the number 287 written on the paper. I thought to myself, what an amazing thing that we were able to get that many people into this little building. That night in the evening service, the pastor announced that they had once again broken their record attendance. He triumphantly declared that 404 had attended that morning! My spirit was crushed. I wondered why he felt that he had to lie to feel good about his ministry. The morning we had was nothing to be ashamed of and no one would have cared that some previous record had been broken. Precious souls were born again, and lives were changed.

I didn't feel like I could return to that church for meetings, even though the pastor asked me to come back. I watched from a distance as they struggled over the next decade or so to maintain that work. It eventually shriveled to just a handful of folks and they closed the doors. Selfish pragmatism is a ministry killer.

A SENSUAL PLEASURE

Without natural affection, trucebreakers, false accusers, incontinent, fierce, despisers of those that are good,

*Traitors, heady, highminded, lovers of pleasures more
than lovers of God.—*2 TIMOTHY 3:3–4

Underneath the layer of a selfish pragmatism lies the root
of a wicked sinful flesh. Unfortunately our flesh didn't get
saved! We are in a daily battle with our flesh. Paul describes this
wrestling match between the flesh and Spirit in Romans 7:14–25:
"*For we know that the law is spiritual: but I am carnal, sold under
sin. For that which I do I allow not: for what I would, that do I not;
but what I hate, that do I. If then I do that which I would not, I
consent unto the law that it is good. Now then it is no more I that
do it, but sin that dwelleth in me. For I know that in me (that is,
in my flesh,) dwelleth no good thing: for to will is present with me;
but how to perform that which is good I find not. For the good that
I would I do not: but the evil which I would not, that I do. Now if I
do that I would not, it is no more I that do it, but sin that dwelleth
in me. I find then a law, that, when I would do good, evil is present
with me. For I delight in the law of God after the inward man: But
I see another law in my members, warring against the law of my
mind, and bringing me into captivity to the law of sin which is in
my members. O wretched man that I am! who shall deliver me
from the body of this death? I thank God through Jesus Christ our
Lord. So then with the mind I myself serve the law of God; but with
the flesh the law of sin.*"

While Satan destroys some lives and ministries through
selfish pragmatism, others are ruined by laziness, distraction,
materialism, and immorality. The devil knows how our flesh
works. He knows what makes our flesh happy and will always

have a large supply of whatever it is that does so to tempt us. The fact that we like something doesn't make it right. Something might make us happy, but it might not be holy.

God sets a pretty high standard in Matthew 5:48: *"Be ye therefore perfect, even as your Father which is in heaven is perfect."* With that challenge in front of us, I'm not sure we can be too strict or have too many standards! When we get saved, the lusts that used to make us happy are to be surrendered to the Lord who can make us holy. *"As obedient children, not fashioning yourselves according to the former lusts in your ignorance: But as he which hath called you is holy, so be ye holy in all manner of conversation: Because it is written, Be ye holy; for I am holy"* (1 Peter 1:14–16).

GOD IS FAR MORE INTERESTED IN OUR HOLINESS THAN HE IS OUR HAPPINESS.

Compromise is taking place today because we don't want to be holy. We don't want to be like Jesus. We don't want to live a Spirit-controlled life, but rather a flesh-controlled life. We argue that this is the twenty-first century, that things have changed, everybody is more worldly minded these days, etc., etc. Titus 2:12 is emphatic: *"Teaching us that, denying ungodliness and worldly lusts, we should live soberly, righteously, and godly in this present world."* In "this" present world! If God wanted us to live any differently now than He did when He wrote that, He would not have stated what He did in a present tense context!

Ask yourself some questions and think biblically about your answers. If Jesus were living on the earth right now…

- Would He attend the movie theater? Rent movies?
- What kind of music would Jesus listen to?
- Would He go on vacation, and if so, where?
- Would He watch television, and if so, what?
- What internet sites would He view or use?
- Would Jesus use text messaging, and if so, how?
- How would Jesus speak to the opposite gender?
- What would Jesus allow Himself to think about?
- What would Jesus wear?
- Where would He shop?
- What would Jesus do on Sundays?
- How would Jesus spend His money?
- How would He spend His time?
- Who would Jesus identify with and in what ways?

There used to be a popular phrase that people displayed in various ways. It read: "What would Jesus do?" We really don't have to wonder about that. We have four Gospels in the New Testament that tell us exactly what Jesus did. And we are commanded to mimic His example!

How would *you* answer the above questions? Be honest. Now carefully think about Colossians 3:17: *"And whatsoever ye do in word or deed, do all in the name of the Lord Jesus, giving thanks to God and the Father by him."* Can you thank God for your answers? Can you do the things you are doing in your life in the name of the Lord Jesus? If not, they must be eliminated. Sensual pleasure is a dangerous component that leads to compromise.

A SUBSTITUTED POWER

Having a form of godliness, but denying the power thereof.—2 TIMOTHY 3:5

Put this book down for a moment and either literally or figuratively walk slowly through the rooms of your house. Where are you? Are you in the living room? Look around. What do you see on the walls? I want you to go through each room of your house and carefully count all of the picture frames that are hanging on the walls that do not have pictures in them. Are you counting?

CHRISTIANITY CAN BECOME A FORM; THEN A FORMALITY; AND FINALLY FORMALISM.

You're saying, "I don't have to do that! We don't have any picture frames on the walls without pictures. How stupid would that be?" Okay, I'll admit that was a bad question. How many pictures do you suppose you have in your house that do not have a frame around them? Probably a lot—in a drawer, in your wallet, in a photo album, the front of your Bible, etc. What's important, the picture or the frame? Paul warns us here that some have only a form (or frame) with nothing inside. Many Christians and many churches today have a form, but the power of God is gone. The glory has departed.

Often when we don't see the results that we think we should have, the fundamentals become a formality, and we begin looking for other methods and other means to grow the church. It isn't working God's way we suppose, so we rationalize to try it our way. When that occurs, we must get our eyes off of the need for success and back on the need for the Scriptures.

DOES PREACHING WORK?

The Bible says it does. *"For the preaching of the cross is to them that perish foolishness; but unto us which are saved it is the power of God. For it is written, I will destroy the wisdom of the wise, and will bring to nothing the understanding of the prudent. Where is the wise? where is the scribe? where is the disputer of this world, hath not God made foolish the wisdom of this world? For after that in the wisdom of God the world by wisdom knew not God, it pleased God by the foolishness of preaching to save them that believe"* (1 Corinthians 1:18–21).

DOES PRAYER WORK?

The Bible says it does. *"Call unto me, and I will answer thee, and shew thee great and mighty things, which thou knowest not"* (Jeremiah 33:3). *"And it shall come to pass, that before they call, I will answer; and while they are yet speaking, I will hear"* (Isaiah 65:24). *"Ask, and it shall be given you; seek, and ye shall find; knock, and it shall be opened unto you: For every one that asketh receiveth; and he that seeketh findeth; and to him that knocketh it shall be opened"* (Matthew 7:7–8). *"And this is the confidence that we have in him, that, if we ask any thing according to his will, he heareth us: And if we know that he hear us, whatsoever we ask, we know that we have the petitions that we desired of him"* (1 John 5:14–15).

DOES GOD HONOR FAITH?

The Bible says He does. *"But without faith it is impossible to please him: for he that cometh to God must believe that he is, and that he is a rewarder of them that diligently seek him"* (Hebrews 11:6). *"Then came the disciples to Jesus apart, and said, Why could not we cast him out? And Jesus said unto them, Because of your unbelief: for verily I say unto you, If ye have faith as a grain of mustard seed, ye shall say unto this mountain, Remove hence to yonder place; and it shall remove; and nothing shall be impossible unto you"* (Matthew 17:19–20).

DOES SOULWINNING WORK?

The Bible says it does. *"They that sow in tears shall reap in joy. He that goeth forth and weepeth, bearing precious seed, shall doubtless come again with rejoicing, bringing his sheaves with him"* (Psalm 126:5–6). *"The fruit of the righteous is a tree of life; and he that winneth souls is wise"* (Proverbs 11:30).

DOES GOD BLESS TITHES AND OFFERINGS?

The Bible says He does. *"Even from the days of your fathers ye are gone away from mine ordinances, and have not kept them. Return unto me, and I will return unto you, saith the Lord of hosts. But ye said, Wherein shall we return? Will a man rob God? Yet ye have robbed me. But ye say, Wherein have we robbed thee? In tithes and offerings. Ye are cursed with a curse: for ye have robbed me, even this whole nation. Bring ye all the tithes into the storehouse, that there may be meat in mine house, and prove me now herewith, saith the Lord of hosts, if I will not open you the windows of heaven, and pour you out a blessing, that there shall not be room enough to receive it"* (Malachi 3:7–10). *"Give, and it shall be given unto you; good measure, pressed down, and shaken together, and running over, shall men give into your bosom. For with the same measure that ye meet withal it shall be measured to you again"* (Luke 6:38). *"But this I say, He which soweth sparingly shall reap also sparingly; and he which soweth bountifully shall reap also bountifully. Every man according as he purposeth in his heart, so let him give; not grudgingly, or of necessity: for God loveth a cheerful giver. And God is able to make all grace abound toward you; that ye, always having all sufficiency in all things, may abound to every good work"* (2 Corinthians 9:6–8).

DOES GOD HONOR FAITHFUL SERVICE?

The Bible says He does. *"A faithful man shall abound with blessings"* (Proverbs 28:20A). *"And let us not be weary in well doing: for in due season we shall reap, if we faint not"* (Galatians 6:9). *"…be thou faithful unto death, and I will give thee a crown of life"* (Revelation 2:10B).

WE ARE ALLOWING EDUCATION TO ELEVATE US TO AN ELITE STATUS OF ENLIGHTENMENT.

It comes down to whether you believe the Book or somebody's blog! Compromise is in full swing when ministries have formalities without the power of God. Services are conducted, sermons are preached, prayers are recited, songs are sung, choirs rehearse, buses are run, youth activities are conducted, the Christian school is in session, the bills are being paid, but "Ichabod" is written over the front door.

In the Old Testament, the Ark of the Covenant was symbolic of God's presence and power. Without the Ark, the children of Israel were in trouble. *"And his daughter in law, Phinehas' wife, was with child, near to be delivered: and when she heard the tidings that the ark of God was taken, and that her father in law and her husband were dead, she bowed herself and travailed; for her pains came upon her. And about the time of her death the women that stood by her said unto her, Fear not; for thou hast born a son. But she answered not, neither did she regard it. And she named the child Ichabod, saying, The glory is departed from Israel: because the ark of God was taken, and because of her father in law and her husband. And she said, The glory is departed from Israel: for the ark of God is taken"* (1 Samuel 4:19–22).

We don't need some rap artist to grow the church—God blesses the preaching of His Word. We don't need some positive thinking mystic to calm our fears—God answers prayer. We don't need some marketing strategy to grow the church—God says Go, Win, Baptize, and Disciple! What we need is not in ourselves, or in some book, or on some blog, or at some seminar. It is in the Person of God! *"Not that we are sufficient of ourselves to think any thing of ourselves; but our sufficiency is of God"* (2 Corinthians 3:5).

We are settling for picture frames today! *"Then he answered and spake unto me, saying, This is the word of the Lord unto Zerubbabel, saying, Not by might, nor by power, but by my spirit, saith the Lord of hosts"* (Zechariah 4:6). Lots of churches have form, formality, and formalism, but Jesus said: *"…without me ye can do nothing"* (John 15:5b).

A SCHOLASTIC PRIDE

Ever learning, and never able to come to the knowledge of the truth.—2 TIMOTHY 3:7

Let me say from the outset here that I am not against education. I started out in ministry teaching in a Christian school. Presently, I teach in a Bible college. I have a bachelor's degree, two Master's degrees, and a PhD in Christian Education. I have spent thousands of hours reading and studying my Bible to try to learn God's heart and God's ways. I have tried to read as much as I can to equip myself with the knowledge of others in order to serve the Lord in a greater way. The Bible admonishes each of us to *"Study to shew thyself approved unto God, a workman that needeth not to be ashamed, rightly dividing the word of truth"* (2 Timothy 2:15).

Scholasticism and intellectualism however are killing us! We are allowing education to elevate us to an elite status of enlightenment. The prophet Isaiah warns us, *"...Thy wisdom and thy knowledge, it hath perverted thee; and thou hast said in thine heart, I am, and none else beside me"* (Isaiah 47:10). Notice the connection in this verse between knowledge and pride. We are instructed to grow in the knowledge of Jesus Christ (see 2 Peter 3:18), but when pride enters the picture, it drives us away from Christ for it is the number one sin on God's hate list (see Proverbs 6:16–17A).

God doesn't choose to use people based on their intelligence or qualifications. In fact, He often can't use those people because if He did, their pride would steal the credit. *"For ye see your calling, brethren, how that not many wise men after the flesh, not many mighty, not many noble, are called: But God hath chosen the foolish things of the world to confound the wise; and God hath chosen the weak things of the world to confound the things which are mighty; And base things of the world, and things which are despised, hath God chosen, yea, and things which are not, to bring to nought things that are: That no flesh should glory in his presence"* (1 Corinthians 1:26–29).

So often the argument for intellectualism and scholasticism is made on the basis of gaining credibility with the world. We want to reach the world with our message, and so we feel in order to do so we must have some credibility. Since education is that recognizable commodity, we tout it as our "in" to the world. In Acts 4, Peter and John had been arrested for preaching. They had gotten the world's attention. The next day as they were questioned, Peter and John attributed all of their power and authority to Jesus Christ and Him alone. No doubt, they got laughed right out of town, right? *"Now when they saw the boldness of Peter and John, and perceived that they were unlearned and ignorant men, they marvelled; and they took knowledge of them, that they had been with Jesus"* (Acts 4:13). The world took notice of Peter and John, not because of their education for they had none, but because they had been with Jesus! Today we have all kinds of education, but the world doesn't seem to notice.

Without question, the Apostle Paul is one of the most gifted and educated men on the pages of the New Testament. He gives us a little of his resumé in Philippians 3:4–6: *"Though I might also have confidence in the flesh. If any other man thinketh that he hath whereof he might trust in the flesh, I more: Circumcised the eighth day, of the stock of Israel, of the tribe of Benjamin, an*

Hebrew of the Hebrews; as touching the law, a Pharisee; Concerning zeal, persecuting the church; touching the righteousness which is in the law, blameless." Mighty impressive! Surely the world will listen to this man. He's the total package—talented, trained, and trusted.

But notice in the next verses how Paul views his resumé: *"But what things were gain to me, those I counted loss for Christ. Yea doubtless, and I count all things but loss for the excellency of the knowledge of Christ Jesus my Lord: for whom I have suffered the loss of all things, and do count them but dung, that I may win Christ, And be found in him, not having mine own righteousness, which is of the law, but that which is through the faith of Christ, the righteousness which is of God by faith: That I may know him, and the power of his resurrection, and the fellowship of his sufferings, being made conformable unto his death"* (Philippians 3:7–10).

Paul knew that if God was going to use Him, it would not be because of his diplomas or degrees. The world has those, but it doesn't have Jesus.

By 1940, fundamentalism was labeled a failure because of its separation from the world in ecclesiastical, social, and intellectual areas. In a convocation message at Fuller Theological Seminary in Pasadena, California in 1948, Harold J. Okenga coined the phrase "new evangelicalism." A short time later, a group of these newly formed new-evangelicals defected from fundamentalism because to the liberal mindset, fundamentalism was associated with ignorance, intolerance, and a reactionary mentality.

Okenga carefully spelled out his dissatisfaction with fundamentalism in three major areas. First, he said that fundamentalists had a wrong attitude toward those who did not hold to every orthodox doctrine. I'm not sure what he meant by a "wrong attitude" but the Bible says in Romans 16:17: *"Now I beseech you, brethren, mark them which cause divisions and offences contrary to the doctrine which ye have learned; and avoid them."*

Second, Okenga stated that fundamentalism had developed a wrong strategy of separation from religious liberalism. He proposed "infiltration" as a correct strategy—that is, putting aside doctrinal differences and looking for areas of agreement and cooperation. This is an interesting and, no doubt to some, an enticing strategy but clearly unbiblical. *"Be ye not unequally yoked together with unbelievers: for what fellowship hath righteousness with unrighteousness? and what communion hath light with darkness? And what concord hath Christ with Belial? or what part hath he that believeth with an infidel? And what agreement hath the temple of God with idols? for ye are the temple of the living God; as God hath said, I will dwell in them, and walk in them; and I will be their God, and they shall be my people. Wherefore come out from among them, and be ye separate, saith the Lord, and touch not the unclean thing; and I will receive you, And will be a Father unto you, and ye shall be my sons and daughters, saith the Lord Almighty"* (2 Corinthians 6:14–18).

GOD DIDN'T SAVE US TO IMPRESS THE WORLD WITH OUR SCHOLASTICISM. HE SAVED US TO IMPACT THE WORLD FOR OUR SAVIOUR!

Third, he said that fundamentalism was obviously wrong because of its wrong results in the battle against liberalism.

Liberalism was taking over all of the mainline denominational schools and new-evangelicalism was designed to recapture denominational leadership. Well, if results are the benchmark of success, then Noah should have scrapped the ark and taken swimming lessons. Joseph should have cursed his brothers and become immoral. Daniel shouldn't have prayed. The three Hebrews should have bowed. John the Baptist should have kept his mouth shut, and Jesus should have come down from the cross! The majority is not the priority.

In an article entitled "Is Evangelical Theology Changing?" published in the *Christian Life* magazine in March of 1956, new evangelicalism listed eight features of their movement. They were as follows:

- A friendly attitude toward science.
- A willingness to re-examine beliefs concerning the work of the Holy Spirit.
- A more tolerant attitude toward varying views on eschatology.
- A shift away from so-called extreme dispensationalism.
- An increased emphasis on scholarship.
- A more definite recognition of social responsibility.
- A re-opening of the subject of biblical inspiration.
- A growing willingness of evangelical theologians to converse with liberal theologians.

Keep in mind that fundamental Baptists have always distinguished themselves first and foremost by their sole allegiance to the Bible as their guide for faith and practice. So why do we need to "re-examine," "be more tolerant," "shift away," "increase emphasis," or "re-open" anything? To do so would without question lead to compromise.

Our scholastic pride causes us to want to sit down and dialogue with the enemies of Christ. King Nebuchadnezzar captured young Daniel and put him in his institution for "higher learning." It was a three-year program, and Daniel was chosen because it was obvious he had what it would take to be a great leader in Babylon. If Daniel had succumbed to his pride, he would have yielded thinking that he could influence the world by his position upon graduation. *"But Daniel purposed in his heart that he would not defile himself with the portion of the king's meat, nor with the wine which he drank: therefore he requested of the prince of the eunuchs that he might not defile himself"* (Daniel 1:8).

Moses as a small child was taken into Egypt by Pharaoh's daughter. Placed in the finest schools, he was trained in the way of the Egyptians (the enemies of God). But, *"By faith Moses, when he was come to years, refused to be called the son of Pharaoh's daughter: Choosing rather to suffer affliction with the people of God, than to enjoy the pleasures of sin for a season; Esteeming the reproach of Christ greater riches than the treasures in Egypt: for he had respect unto the recompense of the reward"* (Hebrews 11:24–26).

SCORNED PRINCIPLES ALWAYS LEAD TO SINFUL PRACTICES.

God didn't save us to impress the world with our scholasticism. He saved us to impact the world for our Saviour!

A SCORNING OF PRINCIPLES

Now as Jannes and Jambres withstood Moses, so do these also resist the truth: men of corrupt minds, reprobate concerning the faith.—2 TIMOTHY 3:8

I am a strong proponent of people using their brain (I think I've already mentioned that). It is important that we learn how to think. We must learn to think biblically and theologically. We must develop common sense and prudence. With our knowledge it is important to develop wisdom and understanding. But we had better think long and hard about turning our backs on the principles of Scripture that our forefathers have lived for and died for. Our generation is quick to dismiss and trample the old paths then come up with something new.

I don't know much about the background or personality of Jannes and Jambres, but the Bible says they "withstood Moses." Numbers 12:3 describes Moses as a meek man. *"(Now the man Moses was very meek, above all the men which were upon the face of the earth.)"* God refers to Moses as His friend in Exodus 33:11A: *"And the LORD spake unto Moses face to face, as a man speaketh unto his friend."* It seems to me that Moses would be an easy leader to follow.

I honestly think that some people rebel for the sake of rebelling. There isn't anything specific they don't like. They just don't want to submit to authority in their life. We have been indoctrinated over the past fifty years to question authority. I realize that some authority is questionable and we may be disappointed in some leaders, but the Bible doesn't give us that loophole. In Hebrews 13:7, God admonishes us to *"Remember them which have the rule over you, who have spoken unto you the word of God: whose faith follow, considering the end of their conversation."* Later in the chapter He informs us that there are eternal ramifications to that submission or lack thereof. *"Obey them that have the rule over you, and submit yourselves: for they watch for your souls, as they that must give account, that they may do it with joy, and not with grief: for that is unprofitable for you"* (Hebrews 13:17).

I would challenge you to find someone in the Bible who rebelled against authority and won. There are many that did so and lost (Lucifer, Adam, Cain, Achan, Absalom, King Saul, and Solomon to name a few). But I can show you some people who submitted to a *wrong* authority and won. Laban mistreated Jacob with respect to his requirements for his daughter Rachel. Jacob however, worked an extra seven years for Laban and God blessed him with Rachel. Joseph was wronged by Potiphar's wife, lied about and thrown in prison. But Joseph served faithfully and God exalted him. David was careful not to touch Saul, God's anointed, even though Saul had lost the blessing of God and was dominated by an evil spirit. David ended up being king and Saul was killed.

We display a sinful arrogance when we think we are smarter than the leaders God has placed over us. To do so is to put ourselves on dangerous ground. *"For rebellion is as the sin of witchcraft, and stubbornness is as iniquity and idolatry"* (1 Samuel 15:23A). Children, watch out when you think you know more than your parents. Church member, watch out when you think you're smarter than your pastor. Preacher, watch out when you think you're smarter than the countless thousands who have served God before you.

Principles from the Word of God that have been loved, taught, and died for are being scorned by this generation. They did the same to the weeping prophet and compromise followed on its heels. *"And they have turned unto me the back, and not the face: though I taught them, rising up early and teaching them, yet they have not hearkened to receive instruction. But they set their abominations in the house, which is called by my name, to defile it. And they built the high places of Baal, which are in the valley of the son of Hinnom, to cause their sons and their daughters to pass through the fire unto Molech; which I commanded them not, neither came it into my mind, that they should do this abomination, to cause Judah to sin"* (Jeremiah 32:33–35). Scorned principles always lead to sinful practices!

A SPURNED PREPARATION

But thou hast fully known my doctrine, manner of life, purpose, faith, longsuffering, charity, patience, Persecutions, afflictions, which came unto me at Antioch, at Iconium, at Lystra; what persecutions I endured: but out of them all the Lord delivered me.
—2 TIMOTHY 3:10–11

Have you ever been in a hurry to wash your clothes? Often as I am out on the road preaching, I need to do my laundry. Usually I will take something with me to study or work on as I head down to some local laundromat. It's hard to study in those places. People are talking, the television is usually blaring, it's either really hot or really cold, the only chairs are of the plastic lawn variety, and there are a lot of really weird people that frequent those places. But no matter how desperate you are to get out of there, you can't hurry the process. That washing machine has a series of cycles for your clothes to go through if they are going to get clean.

I can't tell you how many times in the ministry I have seen compromise come into a church because someone did not allow themselves to be prepared properly. I love Psalm 37:23: *"The steps of a good man are ordered by the LORD: and he delighteth in his way."* We get excited about the destinations that the Lord has planned for us. But God has not only ordered the destination but every step in the process of getting there.

We look at preparation as a waste of time. But how do we know what we need? I chuckle when I hear preachers say: "They didn't teach me that in Bible college!" The truth is they more than likely did; you just didn't think you needed it then. Becoming equipped for ministry is not simply acquiring the principles, but being acquiescent to the process. Spurn the preparation—shortchange the product!

Learning to back a trailer or piece of machinery on the farm was a painful process. Back in those days we cleaned the barn each morning by backing a manure spreader down the center of the barn and shoveling the manure into that manure spreader one shovel full at a time. My dad showed great patience as I would back that spreader a few feet and then get too close to the gutter and have to pull forward to get it straight again. Then back a few more feet and repeat the process until I could get it backed all the way to the end of the barn. But by the time I was a teenager, I think I could have done it with my eyes closed. When you do something every day, 365 days a year, for several years, you get pretty good at the task.

After our first son was born, we bought our first travel trailer and lived in it as we preached revival meetings around the country. I was scheduled to preach a revival in downtown San Francisco. I called the pastor and he told me he would have to be out of town on Saturday evening when we arrived. He informed me there was a gated parking lot right next to the church where we could park our trailer. He said the street was very busy and the gate was rather narrow, so it might be a challenge backing it into that lot.

When we arrived it was pouring rain. I drove up alongside that parking lot as cars whizzed past me on the four-lane street in front of the church. I got out and opened the gate. Sizing it up in the rain, I could see it was indeed narrow (Later, I measured it—we had three inches to spare on either side). I told my wife; "we've got one shot at this. You're going to have to get out and try to stop some of this traffic while I back it in." She looked at me like I was crazy. She said, "You want me to stand out there in the rain?" I informed her that she could either do that, or let me do that and she could back the trailer! She got out and did her best to stop a few cars. I pulled out into the street and in the dark in pouring rain backed that trailer right through the opening on the first shot!

I remember thinking about my dad that night as I unhooked the trailer and got it set up for the week. I would have never been successful had he not patiently allowed me to go through some painful preparation that God knew would come in handy one cold rainy night in San Francisco.

We may not always like the "cycle" we're in, but God has a reason for our being there. To spurn that preparation will cause us to cut corners later in compromise.

A SCARY PERSECUTION

Yea, and all that will live godly in Christ Jesus shall suffer persecution.—2 TIMOTHY 3:12

The Bible is a book of promises. Someone has said that there are over six-hundred promises to the child of God. They will all come to pass because it says in 2 Corinthians 1:20 that "*...all the promises of God in him are yea, and in him Amen, unto the glory of God by us.*"

There are a few promises, however, that I don't like! Verse 12 is one of them. God says all who live godly in Christ Jesus *shall* suffer persecution. The word *shall* indicates a promise that is just as sure as "*For whosoever **shall** call upon the name of the Lord **shall** be saved*" (Romans 10:13). I'll be honest, I don't get excited about persecution. I told Attorney David Gibbs one day: "I'm not afraid to *go* to jail, but I am afraid to be *in* jail." Jail is a rough place. I have been privileged to preach in many of them, but have always been thrilled that I could leave when I was done.

The Bible tells us not to be alarmed when the fiery trials come. "*Beloved, think it not strange concerning the fiery trial which is to try you, as though some strange thing happened unto you: But rejoice, inasmuch as ye are partakers of Christ's sufferings; that, when his glory shall be revealed, ye may be glad also with exceeding joy. If ye be reproached for the name of Christ, happy are ye; for the spirit of glory and of God resteth upon you: on their part he is evil spoken of, but on your part he is glorified"* (1 Peter 4:12–14). We can't expect the world to be on our side and love us for our stand. There is a reason for that: *"If the world hate you, ye know that it hated me before it hated you. If ye were of the world, the world would love his own: but because ye are not of the world, but I have chosen you out of the world, therefore the world hateth you"* (John 15:18–19).

Some of us find it easy to stand as long as it's easy. When our convictions are tested, we compromise rather than suffer. In Luke 14:27, Jesus said: *"And whosoever doth not bear his cross, and come after me, cannot be my disciple."* The cross is an instrument of death and following Christ and obeying His Word means picking it up daily and dying to self. When the attacks come, you can throw down that cross and compromise or you can do what the writer of Hebrews admonished us to do: *"Looking unto Jesus the author and finisher of our faith; who for the joy that was set before him endured the cross, despising the shame, and is set down at the right hand of the throne of God. For consider him that endured such contradiction of sinners against himself, lest ye be wearied and faint in your minds"* (Hebrews 12:2–3).

Compromise is not an event—it's an evolution. Selfish pragmatism, sensual pleasure, substituted power, scholastic pride, scorned principles, spurned preparation, and scary persecution are all components of that evolution. With each attack we are tempted to take out our saw and hack off some of the board containing our convictions. We don't think it matters, but in the end there is nothing left.

FOUR

THE TRICKERY
SATAN: THE MASTER OF MASQUERADE

*And no marvel; for Satan himself is transformed
into an angel of light.*—2 CORINTHIANS 11:14

I t was Halloween night and we were in Danville, Illinois to start a revival the next morning. We parked the trailer at the church as usual, met with the pastor to go over the schedule, and settled in for a little family time. The kids were small and they had been begging us to let them go trick or treating. Growing up on a farm out in the country, my parents never had to explain the good or bad of this event since we weren't stupid enough to want to walk a half a mile to the closest neighbor in a costume just to get a piece of bubble gum.

As young parents, my wife and I weren't really sure what to do. We weren't against the kids getting candy (maybe they would even share) but we didn't really want them getting too excited about the devil's holiday either. So we came up with a strategy that our kids remember and talk about to this day.

71

We went down to Kmart and bought some cheap plastic costumes and brought them back to the trailer. The kids dressed up and I instructed them to go with their mother and I would catch up to them later. They had their little bags to fill with candy as they headed out the trailer door into the church parking lot. Diane marched them in their costumes around the parking lot a couple of times while inside the trailer I made a costume change of my own. (I think this may be where my passion for writing and directing college dramas actually started.) After about ten minutes of walking, they came and knocked on the trailer door. (With their little masks over their faces, I'm not sure they realized that they hadn't gone anywhere.)

I answered the door dressed as a chunky but pleasant old lady. I smiled and talked nicely to the children admiring their costumes while pouring handfuls of candy generously into their little bags. Their eyes were as big as saucers as they stared at me in bewilderment behind my wig, makeup and dress. I closed the door and Diane marched them around the lot a couple more times and again knocked on the door. This time I answered it in a gruff voice and yelled at them from behind my beard and ball cap. After scolding them for bothering me, I again heaped more candy into their bags.

SATAN RARELY ACTS LIKE SATAN: HE ACTS LIKE GOD.

We continued this process for an hour or more as they came back several times to the trailer to meet some "new" occupant but always receiving generous donations of candy. They caught on pretty quickly as my acting skills were good but my costume closet was a bit limited. We all laughed a lot that night and many times since and enjoyed a lot of candy!

Satan has a costume and he doesn't just wear it on Halloween. He has been masquerading since his fall from heaven. The devil knows all about God and in reality wants to replace Him. *"How art thou fallen from heaven, O Lucifer, son of the morning! how art thou cut down to the ground, which didst weaken the nations! For thou hast said in thine heart I will ascend into heaven, I will exalt my throne above the stars of God: I will sit also upon the mount of the congregation, in the sides of the north: I will ascend above the heights of the clouds; I will be like the most High. Yet thou shalt be brought down to hell, to the sides of the pit"* (Isaiah 14:12–15).

Satan knows who God is and tries to masquerade as God. He knows Truth and will do everything he can to change that Truth into a lie and yet present it to us as truth. Everything he does is anti-Christ while all of the time portraying himself as equal to or better than Christ. He does all of this by wearing a beautiful costume.

As we have seen, Truth will stand up to any and every test it is given. In fact, Truth sees right through this masquerade of Satan, pulling the mask from off of his hideous face and shredding his costume to pieces. *"Ye are of your father the devil, and the lusts of your father ye will do. He was a murderer from the beginning, and abode not in the truth, because there is no truth in him. When he speaketh a lie, he speaketh of his own; for he is a liar, and the father of it"* (John 8:44).

Satan rarely acts like Satan—He acts like God. He disguises himself so that we don't recognize that it is him. If we knew it was him and understood that he was out to annihilate us, we would resist him. So, Satan dons his costume and mask and presents himself as truth when in reality there is no truth in him.

The attacks against Christianity down through the centuries have rarely come from pagans. Persecution against God's people has come time and time again from religious groups who declared that they were right and those following the Bible were heretics (check out the Inquisition). Those who opposed Jesus the most were the Pharisees and Sadducees who boasted of their religious systems and rituals. Stephen was stoned to death by religious zealots like Saul of Tarsus who believed that Stephen blasphemed God by following Jesus Christ rather than the law.

Later, the Apostle Paul is also attacked by those he identifies as "false apostles." As he exposes them in 2 Corinthians 11:13–15, he gives us insight into the "costume" of Satan. *"For such are false apostles, deceitful workers, transforming themselves into the apostles of Christ. And no marvel; for Satan himself is transformed into an angel of light. Therefore it is no great thing if his ministers also be transformed as the ministers of righteousness; whose end shall be according to their works."* Satan can't afford to act like Satan if he expects to win the battle against Truth. He has to look and act like God.

Suppose I go into a restaurant for a meal. As the waitress seats me and hands me a menu, she asks: "Can I bring you something to drink?" I respond by saying: "Yes, I would like a Sprite, please." She writes it down and tells me she will be right back. A moment later she sets a glass down in front of me with a straw. The glass is filled with a liquid that is dark brown in color. I would immediately reject it by saying, "Ma'am, I asked for a Sprite." To which she replies: "Oh I'm sorry, my mistake, I thought you said a Coke." I wouldn't have to take a drink of my beverage to know that she brought me the wrong drink. I could tell by looking at it that it was not a Sprite.

But suppose the same waitress comes back and sets a glass down in front of me with water inside. I would probably proceed to place my order and not realize her mistake until I took a drink. Now why would it take me that long to discover the error? Because, Sprite and water "look" alike and I would not be able to discern the difference as easily.

For centuries, the devil has been using religion to destroy religion. Satan could probably rile up enough lost people to pass laws against Christianity. He could get some folks agitated enough to try to outlaw the Bible. But it's a lot easier for him to pull off an "inside job." He costumes his lies and presents them as truth.

The emergent church is a movement that is attracting masses of people today. Relatively unheard of a decade ago, it has taken the world by storm. Younger people in particular are attracted to their charismatic leaders who promote a belief system without a lot of rules or stipulations. While actual meeting places are hard to find, the shelves are stacked with their books and the internet filled with their blogs.

One could define this movement as an informal affiliation of various "Christian" communities globally that desire to revamp

---

1.   Andy Crouch, "The Emergent Mystique," *Christianity Today,* 1 November 2004.
2.   John H. Armstrong, "How I Changed My Mind: Theological Method," *Viewpoint* 7.4, September–October 2003: p. 4.

the church, change the way Christians interact with the culture around them, and reconstruct the truth model. Their leaders tell us that truth is actually hazy, indistinct, and uncertain—perhaps even unknowable. Anyone who stands and declares that they are preaching the truth is considered arrogant. Humility is a prime virtue and anyone who narrow-mindedly preaches only one way to heaven is obviously not humble. Certainty they say is overrated, and we are wise to keep our theology in a constant state of flux.

For example, Brian McLaren, one of their leaders, is quoted in an article called "The Emergent Mystique" as saying, "I don't think we've got the gospel right yet...I don't think the liberals have it right. But I don't think we have it right either. None of us has arrived at orthodoxy."[1] John Armstrong, a former pastor and now conference speaker and author writes, "If there is a foundation in Christian theology, and I believe that there must be, then it is not found in the Church, Scripture, tradition or culture."[2]

Now if you have gotten to this point in this book and are still wondering why I felt the need to write one—here it is! These men are deceivers! Apostates! Heretics! Young preachers and old alike along with a host of God's people are infatuated with this crowd—reading their sermons, devouring their books, following their tweets, and pondering their blogs. God says to curse them!

Let's go to the Truth and let it rip off the costume. Mr. Armstrong says that Scripture is not the foundation of Christian doctrine but Jesus said *"Thy word is truth"* (John 17:17), so I'm going to go with Jesus on this one. McLaren says we don't have the Gospel right yet, but Scripture is emphatic. *"Moreover, brethren, I declare unto you the gospel which I preached unto you, which also ye have received, and wherein ye stand; By which also ye are saved, if ye keep in memory what I preached unto you, unless ye have believed in vain. For I delivered unto you first of all that which I also received, how that Christ died for our sins according to the scriptures; And that he was buried, and that he rose again the third day according to the scriptures"* (1 Corinthians 15:1–4). The Gospel that saves according to the Bible is the death, burial, and resurrection of Jesus Christ.

THE TEACHINGS OF THE EMERGENT CHURCH ARE ABSOLUTE HERESY AND MUST BE REVEALED, REFUTED, AND REJECTED.

Later in his epistle to the church at Galatia, Paul recognizes that Satan has slipped in wearing his costume of light, and proceeds to rip it off. *"I marvel that ye are so soon removed from him that called you into the grace of Christ unto another gospel: Which is not another; but there be some that trouble you, and would pervert the gospel of Christ. But though we, or an angel from heaven, preach any other gospel unto you than that which we have preached unto you, let him be accursed. As we said before, so say I now again, If any man preach any other gospel unto you than that ye have received, let him be accursed. For do I now persuade men, or God? or do I seek to please men? for if I yet pleased men, I*

---

3.   Martin Luther, D. Martin Luther's Werke, Kritische Gesamtausgabe. Briefwechsel, 18 vols. Weimar: Verlag Hermann Bohlaus Nachfolger, 1930–85, 3:81

should not be the servant of Christ. But I certify you, brethren, that the gospel which was preached of me is not after men. For I neither received it of men, neither was I taught it, but by the revelation of Jesus Christ" (Galatians 1:6–12).

The Apostle Paul, under the inspiration of the Holy Spirit, plainly declared the Gospel and warned us under that same inspiration to reject any and all who declare otherwise. For the emergent church to say that truth is unknowable and that we don't have the Gospel right is absolute heresy, and if you rip away the religious costume that they are wearing, you will find Satan himself!

We must not sit idly by and let these false teachings blend into our beliefs. Water and oil don't mix! Too many of God's people today are sitting around in some coffee shop arguing and debating non-essentials while the minds of our young people and new converts are being poisoned by false teachers. This isn't a war over the color of the carpet in the bathroom; this is a war over the content of the Bible!

TRUTH HAS BEEN DETERMINED AND FIXED FOREVER BY THE MIND OF GOD.

I am not a big fan of Martin Luther, but I have pondered the following quotation often. The older I get the less I enjoy being negative. I'm not trying to start a fire, but I believe we have one that needs to be put out. Give some thought to these words before you lay this book aside or more importantly these issues aside:

"If I profess with the loudest of voice and clearest exposition every portion of the Word of God except precisely that little point which the world and the devil are at that moment attacking, I am not confessing Christ, however boldly I may be professing Christ. Where the battle rages, there the loyalty of the soldier is proved; and to be steady on the battlefields besides, is mere flight and disgrace if he flinches at that point."[3]

Satan and his false teachers masquerading as light have chosen a battlefield. With the help of Truth from 2 Corinthians 11, let's make our way to that battlefield and pull off some costumes.

FALSE TEACHERS HAVE A MASQUERADED MINISTRY

For such are false apostles, deceitful workers.
—2 CORINTHIANS 11:13A

The words *false* and *deceitful* are connected to the words *apostles* and *workers.* As stated earlier, Satan is using religion to destroy religion—ministers to destroy ministries.

Rob and Kristen Bell of "Mars Hill" in Grand Rapids, Michigan have this to say in "The Emergent Mystique" article in *Christianity Today* published in November of 2004: "We found ourselves increasingly uncomfortable with church." Kristen says: "It worked for me for a long time, but then it stopped working." The Bells started questioning their assumptions of the Bible itself—discovering the Bible as a human product rather than a product of divine fiat. Kristen adds: "I grew up thinking we've figured out the Bible, that we knew what it means. Now I have no idea what most of it means. And yet I feel like life is big again— like life used to be in black and white, and now it's in color."

First of all, God is very comfortable with church and commands us without apology to get ourselves to the house of God where the man of God declares the Truth of God. *"Not forsaking the assembling of ourselves together, as the manner of some is; but exhorting one another: and so much the more, as ye see the day approaching"* (Hebrews 10:25). This is not the time to be bailing out of the church doors. We are to gather more often as we approach the return of Christ. By the way, in the book of Acts they assembled daily. We are a lot closer to Christ's return than they were and yet we now declare that we don't need to go at all!

The reason Truth to this crowd has become hazy and uncertain is because they have abandoned Bible preaching churches. The church is the institution that God established to keep the Truth preeminent. *"But if I tarry long, that thou mayest know how thou oughtest to behave thyself in the house of God, which is the church of the living God, the pillar and ground of the truth"* (1 Timothy 3:15). Truth and meaning are not determined by our human resources of knowledge or experience. We do not come to certainty through our own feelings or desires. Truth has been determined and fixed forever by the mind of God! *"For ever, O Lord, thy word is settled in heaven"* (Psalm 119:89).

SATAN IS THE MASTER OF MASQUERADE.

God has established Truth and has revealed that Truth in His Word. He established the church to preach the Truth and commands all of us to live in compliance with that Truth. God is not happy with those who tamper with Truth no matter how educated and enlightened they claim to be. He delivers them over to a destructive process.

> *For the wrath of God is revealed from heaven against all ungodliness and unrighteousness of men, who hold the truth in unrighteousness; Because that which may be known of God is manifest in them; for God hath shewed it unto them. For the invisible things of him from the creation of the world are clearly seen, being understood by the things that are made, even his eternal power and Godhead; so that they are without excuse: Because that, when they knew God, they glorified him not as God, neither were thankful; but became vain in their imaginations, and their foolish heart was darkened. Professing themselves to be wise, they became fools, And changed the glory of the uncorruptible God into an image made like to corruptible man, and to birds, and four-footed beasts, and creeping things. Wherefore God also gave them up to uncleanness through the lusts of their own hearts, to dishonour their own bodies between themselves: Who changed the truth of God into a lie, and worshipped and served the creature more than the Creator, who is blessed for ever. Amen.*—ROMANS 1:18–25

When a minister or ministry questions and tampers with the truth of God's Word, you have a masqueraded ministry. Paul says in Romans 16:17, *"Now I beseech you, brethren, mark them which cause divisions and offences contrary to the doctrine which ye have learned; and avoid them."* The Bible says "avoid" them.

That doesn't mean to just get out of their churches. It means quit reading their sermons, subscribing to their websites, and copying their methods. Avoid them!

FALSE TEACHERS HAVE A MASTERFUL MENTOR

And no marvel; for Satan himself is transformed into an angel of light.—2 CORINTHIANS 11:14

Don't lose sight of the real enemy here. It is easy to focus on denominations, movements, churches, and preachers, but the chief foe is Satan himself. He is the master of the masquerade—he has many costumes from which to choose. Earlier in 2 Corinthians 11, Paul shares his heart with the Corinthian believers: *"For I am jealous over you with godly jealousy: for I have espoused you to one husband, that I may present you as a chaste virgin to Christ. But I fear, lest by any means, as the serpent beguiled Eve through his subtilty, so your minds should be corrupted from the simplicity that is in Christ"* (2 Corinthians 11:2–3). Paul uses the term "any means" when describing Satan's attempt to destroy.

THE DEVIL CAN MAKE HIS WEEDS LOOK JUST LIKE GOD'S WHEAT.

In 1 Thessalonians 3:5, Paul reiterates this concern: *"For this cause, when I could no longer forbear, I sent to know your faith, lest by some means the tempter have tempted you, and our labour be in vain."* Here he chooses to use the term "some means" again indicating the multiplicity of fiery darts. The means to the end is not important to the wicked one. In his heart, Lucifer probably hates religion and even the smell of it, but doesn't mind using it to camouflage the Truth.

I have played and watched enough sports in my life to know that it is when you underestimate the competition that you lose. We must not make that mistake with Satan. He is a powerful and intelligent creature who knows what he is doing. He's not God, but he was created by God and endowed with intelligence and beauty.

> *Moreover the word of the LORD came unto me, saying, Son of man, take up a lamentation upon the king of Tyrus, and say unto him, thus saith the LORD GOD; Thou sealest up the sum, full of wisdom, and perfect in beauty. Thou hast been in Eden the garden of God; every precious stone was thy covering, the sardius, topaz, and the diamond, the beryl, the onyx, and the jasper, the sapphire, the emerald, and the carbuncle, and gold: the workmanship of thy tabrets and of thy pipes was prepared in thee in the day that thou was created. Thou art the anointed cherub that covereth; and I have set thee so: thou wast upon the holy mountain of God; thou hast walked up and down in the midst of the stones of fire. Thou wast perfect in thy ways from the day that thou was created, till iniquity was found in thee. By the multitude of thy merchandise they have filled the midst of thee with violence, and thou hast sinned: therefore I will cast thee as profane out of the mountain of God: and I will destroy thee, O covering cherub, from the*

midst of the stones of fire. Thine heart was lifted up because of thy beauty, thou hast corrupted thy wisdom by reason of thy brightness: I will cast thee to the ground, I will lay thee before kings, that they may behold thee. Thou hast defiled thy sanctuaries by the multitude of thine iniquities, by the iniquity of thy traffick; therefore will I bring forth a fire from the midst of thee, it shall devour thee, and I will bring thee to ashes upon the earth in the sight of all them that behold thee.
—EZEKIEL 28:11–18

Remember, Satan acts like God and he can make himself look like God. Do you recall the time Moses and Aaron were sent by God to Pharaoh? They were a bit skeptical about this meeting so God gave them a sign to show Pharaoh. The sign was nothing short of a miracle, but lo and behold the magicians of Egypt were able to duplicate the act!

And the LORD spake unto Moses, and unto Aaron, saying, When Pharaoh shall speak unto you, saying, Shew a miracle for you: then thou shalt say unto Aaron, Take thy rod, and cast it before Pharaoh, and it shall become a serpent. And Moses and Aaron went in unto Pharaoh, and they did so as the LORD had commanded: and Aaron cast down his rod before Pharaoh, and before his servants, and it became a serpent. Then Pharoah also called the wise men and the sorcerers: now the magicians of Egypt, they also did in like manner with their enchantments. For they

cast down every man his rod, and they became serpents.
—EXODUS 7:8–12A

One of the first crops that we always planted on the farm was oats. You could plant them early because they could survive heavy rains or even light frost. When the oats came up, it was beautiful. A sea of green would contrast the dead brown shrubs and trees still affected by the winter months.

The oats would grow to about eighteen inches and then develop heads on the ends of the green blades. About that time, it seemed you could look out over those fields and one morning there would be yellow weeds in patches all over that field. We called it golden rod. It was a weed that when it grew up looked just like the oats until it developed it's flower or seed. Then it was obvious. We would have to walk those fields and pull those weeds or they would spread and take over the crop.

The devil is good at making the wheat and the weeds look the same. *"Then Jesus sent the multitudes away, and went into the house: and his disciples came unto him, saying, Declare unto us the parable of the tares of the field. He answered and said unto them, He that soweth the good seed is the Son of man; The field is the world; the good seed are the children of the kingdom; but the tares are the children of the wicked one: The enemy that sowed them is the devil; the harvest is the end of the world; and the reapers are the angels. As therefore the tares are gathered and burned in the fire; so shall it be in the end of this world. The Son of man shall send forth his angels, and they shall gather out of his kingdom all things that offend, and them which do iniquity; And shall cast them into a furnace of fire: there shall be wailing and gnashing of teeth. Then shall the righteous shine forth as the sun in the kingdom of their Father. Who hath ears to hear, let him hear"* (Matthew 13:36–43).

The false teachers of our day are being mentored by a powerful and intelligent marvel. We need to understand our enemy or we will underestimate him. We don't have to fear him or be intimidated because, *"Ye are of God, little children, and have overcome them: because greater is he that is in you, than he that is in the world"* (1 John 4:4).

FALSE TEACHERS HAVE A MANUFACTURED METAMORPHOSIS

…transforming themselves into the apostles of Christ
—2 Corinthians 11:13b

These people have not been transformed by the power of God through the Gospel but are transforming "themselves." I was sitting in my eighth grade General Science class one day when the teacher suddenly used a word I had never heard before: "metamorphosis!" I thought, what kind of a dinosaur are we going to study today? The teacher pulled out "Exhibit A." It was a large jar and inside was a stick with a fuzzy bump about half way up. We crowded around the lab table as he explained a process that was already familiar to all of us. The caterpillar forms a cocoon around himself. Inside metamorphosis takes place (a change of form) and in time he emerges as a beautiful butterfly!

That is exactly what takes place at the moment of salvation—a change of form or metamorphosis! *"Therefore if any man be in Christ, he is a new creature: old things are passed away; behold, all things are become new"* (2 Corinthians 5:17). Salvation is not a reformation but rather a regeneration. God doesn't fix up the old man—he throws the old away and makes all things new.

Man is incapable of manufacturing his own metamorphosis though he tries. *"Brethren, my heart's desire and prayer to God for Israel is, that they might be saved. For I bear them record that they have a zeal of God, but not according to knowledge. For they being ignorant of God's righteousness, and going about to establish their own righteousness, have not submitted themselves unto the righteousness of God. For Christ is the end of the law for righteousness to every one that believeth"* (Romans 10:1–4). Paul states it this way later in Ephesians 2:8–9: *"For by grace are ye saved through faith, and that not of yourselves: it is the gift of God: Not of works, lest any man should boast."* Our works may be impressive to us and those around us but they are no match for the finished work of Christ on the cross. *"Not by works of righteousness which we have done, but according to his mercy he saved us, by the washing of regeneration, and renewing of the Holy Ghost; Which he shed on us abundantly through Jesus Christ our Saviour"* (Titus 3:5–6). Paul told the church at Galatia, *"I do not frustrate the grace of God: for if righteousness come by the law, then Christ is dead in vain"* (Galatians 2:21).

The Pharisees were an amazing group of men in the time of Jesus. On the outside they had a manufactured metamorphosis that could fool anyone—anyone except God. In Luke 18:12, a Pharisee boasts in his prayer: *"I fast twice in the week, I give tithes of all that I possess."* He already has most of us beaten! In

Philippians 3:6, Paul is recalling his life as a Pharisee prior to his conversion and remarks: *"…touching the righteousness which is in the law, blameless."* These Pharisees kept over 400 laws contained in the Old Testament Torah. In fact, I am told that they had the law memorized! They literally had a rule for everything and didn't dare violate a single one. They were revered wherever they went and held up as highly religious and godly.

Until they met Jesus! The Lord reserved his harshest sermon for this manufactured metamorphosis.

> *Woe unto you, scribes and Pharisees, hypocrites! for ye pay tithe of mint and anise and cummin, and have omitted the weightier matters of the law, judgment, mercy, and faith: these ought ye to have done, and not to leave the other undone. Ye blind guides, which strain at a gnat, and swallow a camel. Woe unto you, scribes and Pharisees, hypocrites! for ye make clean the outside of the cup and of the platter, but within they are full of extortion and excess. Thou blind Pharisee, cleanse first that which is within the cup and platter, that the outside of them may be clean also. Woe unto you, scribes and Pharisees, hypocrites! for ye are like unto whited sepulchres, which indeed appear beautiful outward, but are within full of dead men's bones, and of all uncleanness. Even so ye also outwardly appear righteous unto men, but within ye are full of hypocrisy, and iniquity. Woe unto you, scribes and Pharisees, hypocrites! because ye build the tombs of the prophets, and garnish the sepulchres of the righteous, And say, If*

*we had been in the days of our fathers, we would not have
been partakers with them in the blood of the prophets.
Wherefore ye be witnesses unto yourselves, that ye are
the children of them which killed the prophets. Fill ye
up then the measure of your fathers. Ye serpents, ye
generation of vipers, how can ye escape the damnation
of hell?*—MATTHEW 23:23–33

Manufactured metamorphosis ends up in Hell. Why
pretend to be genuine when authentic regeneration is available
through Jesus Christ. Hell will not be less hot for those who
pretend. It might be hotter because they have, as the blind, led
the blind.

FALSE TEACHERS HAVE A MALFUNCTIONED MISSION

…whose end shall be according to their works.
—2 CORINTHIANS 11:15B

Every movement that questions God and rejects the Bible
ends up the same way. *"For we can do nothing against the truth"*
(2 Corinthians 13:8A). Jesus warns in John 12:48, *"He that rejecteth
me, and receiveth not my words, hath one that judgeth him: the
word that I have spoken, the same shall be his judge in the last day."*
No one will be judged by what is written in this book, but all of
us will be judged by what God says in His.

Read carefully what God says about the false teacher
through the Apostle Peter:

The Lord knoweth how to deliver the godly out of temptations, and to reserve the unjust unto the day of judgment to be punished: But chiefly them that walk after the flesh in the lust of uncleanness, and despise government. Presumptuous are they, selfwilled, they are not afraid to speak evil of dignities. Whereas angels, which are greater in power and might, bring not railing accusation against them before the Lord. But these, as natural brute beasts, made to be taken and destroyed, speak evil of the things that they understand not; and shall utterly perish in their own corruption; And shall receive the reward of unrighteousness, as they that count it pleasure to riot in the day time. Spots they are and blemishes, sporting themselves with their own deceivings while they feast with you; Having eyes full of adultery, and that cannot cease from sin; beguiling unstable souls: an heart they have exercised with covetous practices; cursed children: Which have forsaken the right way, and are gone astray, following the way of Balaam the son of Bosor, who loved the wages of unrighteousness; But was rebuked for his iniquity: the dumb ass speaking with man's voice forbad the madness of the prophet. These are wells without water, clouds that are carried with a tempest; to whom the mist of darkness is reserved for ever. For when they speak great swelling words of vanity, they allure through the lusts of the flesh, through much wantonness, those that were clean escaped from them who live in error. While they promise them liberty, they themselves are the servants of corruption: for of whom a man is overcome, of the same is he brought in bondage. For if after they have escaped the pollutions of the world through the knowledge of the Lord and Saviour Jesus Christ, they are again entangled therein, and overcome, the latter end is worse with them than the beginning. For it had been better for them not to have known the way of righteousness, than, after they have known it, to turn from the holy commandment delivered unto them. But it is happened unto them according to the true proverb, The dog is turned to his own vomit again; and the sow that was washed to her wallowing in the mire.—2 PETER 2:9–22

False teachers look good and sound good, but it is impossible for them to do good. They think they are accomplishing good things but the standard is God and the Truth of His Word. They reject the God of the Bible and the Truth He declares, thus nothing eternally good can come from their ministry. We can choose to believe whatever we want and walk according to whatever we choose, but the standard of judgment is already in place. *"Rejoice, O young man, in thy youth; and let thy heart cheer thee in the days of thy youth, and walk in the ways of thine heart, and in the sight of thine eyes: but know thou, that for all these things God will bring thee into judgment"* (Ecclesiastes 11:9).

Solomon sums it up well in the last two verses of Ecclesiastes: *"Let us hear the conclusion of the whole matter: Fear God, and keep his commandments: for this is the whole duty of man. For God shall bring every work into judgment, with every secret thing, whether it be good, or whether it be evil"* (Ecclesiastes 12:13–14). As I have stated before, it all boils down to what you do with Truth.

As a freshman in high school, I tried out for the freshman football team. We went through the usual two-a-day drills where everyone dies in the summer heat. I made the team and the starting line-up as the right tackle on offense. Those coaches in the Midwest loved the farm boys because even though we weren't very big, they knew we had been throwing hundred pound hay bales around all summer.

Our first game was an away game and I was pumped. I couldn't wait to get on the field and experience the thrill of victory. We drove that thirty miles and went into the locker room and dressed for the game. We came out for warm-ups, listened to the national anthem, and lined up to receive the kick-off. After the run-back, I jogged on to that field with my offensive teammates for the first play of my high school career. In the huddle, our quarterback Don Kwapil called an end sweep for our running back Dave Chingway around the left end.

I was crushed. My first play at the right tackle position and we were running the ball the other way. I didn't have to do anything on this particular play except brush block the guy in front of me (he was not going to be able to make the play anyway) and run across the secondary and try to pick off a safety at the end of the run if I could. We broke the huddle and I turned to take my position. When I got up to the line, the defensive tackle was already down on all fours in front of me. His muscles were glistening with sweat; he was breathing heavily; and making a grunting noise. I thought, "What's he so upset about? I'm the one that ought to be mad—they're running the play the other way!"

As I got down in my stance and looked through the flimsy two-barred facemask of my helmet at him, I could tell that he was already shaving as he had about a two day growth of beard. He looked too old to be a freshman! I figured he probably failed a grade or two and so probably wasn't smart enough to know what he was doing on the football field either. About that time, Kwapil began barking the signals and the ball was snapped. My whole world and the rest of my life suddenly changed.

Because I was simply supposed to get in his way for a split second and run down field, when the ball was snapped, I stood straight up figuring he would run into me. He shot across the line of scrimmage as if out of a cannon and brought his right forearm up underneath my chinstrap with one powerful movement. Upon contact, he didn't stop but pushed upward knocking my helmet clean off of my head. After knocking me silly, he had the audacity to run past me and make the tackle on poor Chingway five yards deep in the backfield about the same time he was getting the hand-off.

As I stood there in bewilderment, I felt something trickling from the side of my mouth. As I slid my tongue around my mouth to check out the source of this red liquid now coming from my head, I suddenly felt something missing! Indeed, I was missing something all right—my two front teeth! My two front teeth were lying on the ground in the dirt in front of me. The first play of my life and I had given my two front teeth for Watertown High School. In that split second, I made a decision. Football was a tough game and I was going to have to either quit or get tough. I decided on the latter, went back in the huddle, and started hitting defensive tackles before they could hit me.

As a result of that experience, I have lived with plastic in my mouth since I was fourteen. Losing those teeth put pressure on the teeth around them and so more plastic has been added over the years. False teeth have been a part of my life for a long time. I don't really think about it all that much though. I have quite a number of false teeth in my mouth but they function just like my real teeth. I have to brush them every day, I eat with them, smile with them, and go to the dentist every so often to make sure they are in good order, just like I do with my real teeth. But they are fake! They're phony, plastic, and artificial!

I've never had a dentist look in my mouth and not immediately recognize which of my teeth are real and which ones are plastic. When God looks at ministry and ministers, he knows the real from the fake. Satan is good at making his work look genuine. He is the master of masquerade—the king of costuming—the height of hypocrisy—and a phenomenal phony. The Bible commands us to "prove all things." Test it with Truth. Hold it up to the Light. Satan may have a fancy costume of light but that doesn't mean we have to live in the dark. *"Thy word is a lamp unto my feet, and a light unto my path"* (Psalm 119:105).

F I V E

THE TARGET
THE BATTLE IS FOR TRUTH

And judgment is turned away backward, and
justice standeth afar off: for truth is fallen in the
street, and equity cannot enter.—ISAIAH 59:14

When my wife and I first got married, we went to work in a local church with a Christian school. We loved it and enjoyed the ministry opportunities that God gave us both there and while I was out preaching as an evangelist as often as I could. We weren't making much money in those days—together we made one hundred dollars a week. (This was back in the Old Testament.) Thus, our recreation and entertainment was limited. One day, I saw a dart board on sale at the store. I had never thrown darts but it looked like fun. I bought the dart board, took it home, and hung it on the wall in our apartment.

Being competitive by nature, I began to try to master the art of throwing darts. I would write down my scores and get very frustrated when I couldn't beat my previous best. Diane got frustrated when I missed the whole board and the dart was sticking in the wall! The very center of that dart board had a very small circle called the bull's eye. It was worth fifty points. I tried and tried to hit that spot but don't recall ever hitting that bull's eye. I got to where I could get twenty points any time I wanted, but I never could hit that little round red circle in the middle.

Satan has an array of fiery darts in his arsenal, and he uses them with great skill. He aims at each of us often; he tries to destroy churches and ministries; but his main focus is on the bull's eye. Have you noticed that the name Jesus Christ seems to set off a firestorm of controversy today? Our culture and sadly many religious people avoid that name like the plague. You can mention God and even pray to God publicly, but don't you dare pray in Jesus' name. We don't want His name even associated with His birthday anymore.

I don't think I really understood how angry a person could get over that name until one day I was preaching in a rescue mission. The old building in the inner city was a haven for many of the people who lived on the streets or in poor accommodations. I was thrilled with the opportunity to preach the Gospel. I was surprised to find that the building was packed with two groups of people. To my left in the auditorium sat people who came to those services much like we would go to church. They were born again people who really did love the Lord and loved preaching. They sang enthusiastically and listened intently to God's Word. Many of them would shout "Amen" as I preached.

To my right, was another group of people. These had come off of the streets to get a free meal and a warm bed for the night. They were not particularly interested in hearing a sermon. The service was more or less something they endured in order to get what they needed physically. Their faces showed the effects of sin and no doubt most had nothing in this life but the clothes on their backs. Most never looked up at me but a few listened curiously.

I sensed the Spirit of God working and enjoyed liberty to preach the Gospel until I declared that Jesus Christ was the Son of God; the promised Messiah; and the Saviour of the world. A man jumped from his seat to my right and began to curse. He cursed me which was a little scary in itself, but then he began to curse Jesus Christ. One of the workers coaxed him to the back of the room where he continued his tirade for some time while I endeavored to finish my message. At the invitation several came to trust Christ and I enjoyed for a few moments some good fellowship with some of those dear Christians of the inner city.

Then this man, who had been cursing, broke loose from those who were trying to help him and came angrily to where I was standing at the front of the building. He laid into me once more cursing and blasphemously attacking Jesus Christ. I kindly told him that he had the right to reject Christ but that one day he along with everyone else would bow his knee and with his tongue confess that Jesus Christ is Lord. Men at that point had to physically restrain him or I believe he would have tried to kill me. He hated Jesus Christ with every ounce of his body.

Jesus Christ is the target because Jesus Christ is the Truth. *"In the beginning was the Word, and the Word was with God, and the Word was God. The same was in the beginning with God. All things were made by him; and without him was not any thing made that was made. In him was life; and the life was the light of men. And the light shineth in darkness; and the darkness comprehended it not"* (John 1:1–5). (Interestingly, I am sitting in an airport typing this and a moment ago, I pulled out my Bible to type accurately those verses. As soon as I opened my Bible, a lady sitting across from me packed up her stuff and moved to a section across the terminal!)

Satan hates Jesus Christ because He holds the position that Lucifer wants. Satan according to Isaiah 14 wanted to ascend and be exalted to a position equal to the most High. God said, "No way!" Colossians 1:13–19 tells us why: *"Who hath delivered us from the power of darkness, and hath translated us into the kingdom of his dear Son: In whom we have redemption through his blood,*

EROSION OF TRUTH LEADS TO ERADICATION OF TRUTH.

even the forgiveness of sins: Who is the image of the invisible God, the firstborn of every creature: For by him were all things created, that are in heaven, and that are in earth, visible and invisible, whether they be thrones, or dominions, or principalities, or powers: all things were created by him, and for him.: And he is before all things, and by him all things consist. And he is the head of the body, the church: who is the beginning, the firstborn from the dead; that in all things he might have the preeminence. For it pleased the Father that in him should all fullness dwell."

The moment Jesus was born in Bethlehem He was the target. Thousands of little children under the age of two were slaughtered as Satan hurled his darts in the direction of the bull's eye. In Matthew 4, Satan got really close to the "dart board" as he personally tempted the Lord Jesus to sin. Again, he missed! In John 14:6B Jesus declares: *"I am the way, the truth, and the life.*" When Jesus Christ came to this earth, His life put the Truth in full view. *"And the Word was made flesh, and dwelt among us, (and we beheld his glory, the glory as of the only begotten of the Father,) full of grace and truth"* (John 1:14). When He stood before Pilate, Jesus spelled out clearly what His mission on earth was: *"Pilate therefore said unto him, Art thou a king then? Jesus answered, Thou sayest that I am a king. To this end was I born, and for this cause came I into the world, that I should bear witness unto the truth…"* (John 18:37).

It is this Truth that changes lives! Truth delivers souls from the bondage of sin and translates them into the kingdom of God's Son. Truth releases people from Satan's grip and sets them free to live eternally and abundantly. *"And ye shall know the truth, and the truth shall make you free"* (John 8:32). Truth is the bull's eye upon which Satan has his eye. He will not rest from his warfare against that Truth until he is ultimately cast into a lake of fire forever. Anyone who believes that Truth, preaches that Truth, builds on that Truth, defends that Truth, and lives that Truth is part of that target. That's why the Bible is under so much attack—"thy word is truth." That's why Bible preaching churches are under attack.

> TRUTH IS THE BULL'S EYE UPON WHICH SATAN HAS HIS EYE.

While Satan is powerful, we must keep in mind the last chapter—his trickery. He is subtle and rather than simply destroy the truth, he will "change the truth into a lie." This is why we must be so careful with Scripture and keep studying it diligently. We dare not rely on our own wisdom but always go back to God's Word to make sure that we have the Truth and not a lie disguised as Truth. *"Now we have received, not the spirit of the world, but the spirit which is of God; that we might know the things that are freely given to us of God. Which things also we speak, not in the words which man's wisdom teacheth, but which the Holy Ghost teacheth; comparing spiritual things with spiritual"* (1 Corinthians 2:12–13).

You and I can't outsmart Satan. We can't out-muscle him. We can't out-think him. We can't out-man him. But we can out-Truth him! Jesus simply "out-Truthed" Satan in Matthew 4. Your willpower and man power will not work—you need Truth power!

We are living in a post-modern era. While we enjoy many things in our twenty-first century world, postmodernism presents some challenges that must be fought with Truth. We must not compromise Truth for that is the very target of the age. Satan is eroding at the Truth in order to eradicate the Truth. Little by little Truth is being trampled in our streets and many of God's people are unaware or unconcerned about what is happening not only in our culture but in our churches!

Reading Isaiah 59:3–14, one would think that the prophet Isaiah was writing an editorial piece for *USA Today*.

> *For your hands are defiled with blood, and your fingers with iniquity; your lips have spoken lies, your tongue hath muttered perverseness. None calleth for justice, nor any pleadeth for truth: they trust in vanity, and speak lies; they conceive mischief, and bring forth iniquity. They hatch cockatrice' eggs, and weave the spider's web: he that eateth of their eggs dieth, and that*

which is crushed breaketh out into a viper. Their webs shall not become garments, neither shall they cover themselves with their works: their works are works of iniquity, and the act of violence is in their hands. Their feet run to evil, and they make haste to shed innocent blood; their thoughts are thoughts of iniquity; wasting and destruction are in their paths. The way of peace they know not; and there is no judgment in their goings: they have made them crooked paths: whosoever goeth therein shall not know peace. Therefore is judgment far from us, neither doth justice overtake us: we wait for light, but behold obscurity; for brightness, but we walk in darkness. We grope for the wall like the blind, and we grope as if we had no eyes: we stumble at noon day as in the night; we are in desolate places as dead men. We roar all like bears, and mourn sore like doves: we look for judgment, but there is none; for salvation, but it is far off from us. For our transgressions are multiplied before thee, and our sins testify against us: for our transgressions are with us; and as for our iniquities, we know them; In transgressing and lying against the LORD, *and departing away from our God, speaking oppression and revolt, conceiving and uttering from the heart words of falsehood. And judgment is turned away backward, and justice standeth afar off: for truth is fallen in the street, and equity cannot enter.*

Truth is falling today. We are told in our postmodern world that truth cannot be known, that all truth is relative. There is no true or false, right or wrong, winners and losers. We must tolerate and respect all views and hold all of them up equally as truth. It is now asserted that external absolute truth—that is, truth that is true for all people in all places at all times—cannot be known through reason or science, because truth is non-existent or unknowable. We do not fear error today. Our only fear in the postmodern world is intolerance. Open-mindedness is the highest virtue of man today.

This thinking would be humorous if it weren't so dangerous and ultimately damning. Years ago I attended a pee-wee baseball game. My twin nephews were on one of the teams and like a good uncle I went to support them. The game was as boring as watching paint dry with countless errors and strikeouts. Suddenly after several innings, miraculously the team that my nephews were on scored a run! I jumped from my seat in the bleachers and began to cheer like a wild man. A couple seconds into my euphoria I realized that I was the only one standing with my mouth open. Everyone had turned and was looking at me like I was Osama bin Laden. I sheepishly sat down, looked at my sister-in-law and said: "What was that all about?" She whispered: "Oh, we don't keep score." I thought, "Don't keep score? Why are we here? Why play the game?"

> CAPITAL "T" TRUTH HAS BEEN REPLACED BY SMALL LETTER "t" TRUTH.

We don't want anyone to lose today. We no longer use the word "fail" in our schools. Everyone makes the cheerleading team because we don't want anyone to be disappointed. This may sound a little harsh, but again I am merely going "to the law and to the testimony." If you die with Jesus Christ as your personal Saviour—you win. If you die without Jesus Christ as your Saviour—you lose! *"He that hath the Son hath life; and he that hath not the Son of God hath not life"* (1 John 5:12). There is a true and there is a false. There is right and there is wrong. Some win and some lose.

When I was a teenager back in the 1960s, the catchphrase "do your own thing" became very popular. Dress standards suddenly changed as people dressed or undressed as they pleased ("streaking" in public became very popular). Music changed drastically as any standards or rules were ignored. Morals and ethics began to change. But what was more subtle was the right to "think your own thing." Any and all kinds of thinking became acceptable no matter how absurd they would have sounded earlier.

Bumper stickers appeared with the words, "God is dead." German philosopher Nietzsche's antinomianism was sweeping western culture. "Values Clarification" was nothing more than an assurance that all moral values were relative and thus acceptable. The outgrowth of all this was epistemological relativity; that is, people can only know truth from their experience. This made all truth relative. Suddenly, we couldn't talk about Truth; we could only talk about what was true for you and true for me.

Have you noticed that it's hard to find a good argument anymore? People tolerate every view and thus will defend nothing. You can explain the Gospel to some people and they will smile and say, "That's very nice, I'm glad you believe that." When you ask them if they would like to believe it, they smile and let you know they believe just the opposite. All roads lead to heaven because all truth is relative. The problem is, Jesus said: "I am the way." That simple statement is not tolerant of any other way.

By the time we turned the page of the calendar into the twenty-first century, Capital "T" Truth (Absolute Truth) had been replaced by small letter "t" truth (relative truth). The bull's eye had been penetrated by Satan's dart.

Moral relativity results in chaos and confusion because without absolutes no one can determine right from wrong. Laws become vague and the court system cannot discern justice. All kinds of filth is now protected by our "freedom of speech." Politicians all want to be known as moderate and bi-partisan. We stand for nothing, protect everything, and fall for anything. God declares that we are in trouble: *"Woe unto them that call evil good, and good evil; that put darkness for light, and light for darkness; that put bitter for sweet, and sweet for bitter! Woe unto them that are wise in their own eyes, and prudent in their own sight!"* (Isaiah 5:20–21).

MAN TRUSTS HIS OWN SELFISH LUSTS OVER GOD'S SOVEREIGN LOVE.

This relativism has now permeated ministry. We are told by the emergent church leaders that to be declarative in our preaching about Truth is to be arrogant. We are removing the pulpit from the church auditorium because it's too authoritative and creates a barrier between the preacher and his people. We shouldn't wear a tie when we preach because that too, symbolizes authority. "Thus saith the Lord" is divisive. Preaching is being replaced with dialogue, concerts, and drama. Isaiah wouldn't get too many invites to our churches today. *"Cry aloud, spare not, lift up thy voice like a trumpet, and shew my people their transgression, and the house of Jacob their sins"* (Isaiah 58:1).

In 2001, Stanley Grenz and John Franke published a book entitled "Beyond Foundationalism" with the subtitle: "Shaping Theology in a Postmodern Context." Published in 2001, their goal in this book is to contextualize Christianity. They have decided that since categories and paradigms in the modern world are in collapse, Christianity needs to be re-thought, revised, and adapted to stay relevant in a changing world. Since culture is in a constant state of flux, Christian theology must also be in a constant state of transition. No issue, according to them, is to be regarded as "finally settled." (Somebody hasn't read Psalm 119:89 lately!)

People are confused today because we are not providing direction. God likens us to sheep and on our own we will go astray because our "own way" is to go astray. Jesus provides the key to the problem as He describes it in Matthew 9:36: *"But when he saw the multitudes, he was moved with compassion on them, because they fainted, and were scattered abroad, as sheep having no shepherd."*

Fainting and scattered—why? Because they had no shepherd! People need Truth to guide them and that is exactly why God has given us His Word.

God let the children of Israel wander around in the wilderness for a time to teach them a very important lesson. They thought that they were smarter than God. They supposed that His commandments were old-fashioned and it was time to be liberated. So, God gave them a taste of what it's like to live without absolute Truth to prove His point. *"And he humbled thee, and suffered thee to hunger, and fed thee with manna, which thou knewest not, neither did thy fathers know; that he might make thee know that man doth not live by bread only, but by every word that proceedeth out of the mouth of the* LORD *doth man live"* (Deuteronomy 8:3).

We have a very serious choice to make. Relativism is in vogue today. Tolerance is the buzzword of our culture. Our world has accepted what I like to refer to as "designer" truth. It's popular, fashionable, trendy, and acceptable to all. The Bible speaks of what I will refer to as "discovered" truth. It's old fashioned because it's been around forever—literally. It is absolute, fixed, and eternal. It doesn't need to be changed, altered, or tweaked to fit anything or anyone because it's perfect. We need to conform to it rather than it conforming to us.

Amazingly to me, but not to God, the Apostle Paul deals with this very problem in 2 Timothy 4. We saw earlier the evolution of compromise from 2 Timothy 3, and I again remind you that he closed that chapter with drawing our focus back to *"all scripture"* that makes us wise and throughly furnishes us. Now in the first five verses of chapter 4 the Holy Spirit of God contrasts "designer truth" with "discovered Truth." Remember: designer truth is small letter "t" truth referring to "relative truth." Capital "T" truth refers to absolute Truth and we refer to it as "discovered Truth."

First, let's allow God to expose "designer truth."

DESIGNER TRUTH IS AN EVOLVING TRUTH

In verse 3, Paul says: *"For the time will come when they will not endure sound doctrine."* The truth or doctrine that God has established in his Word is rejected and cast aside. The Bible is considered old-fashioned, out of touch, and irrelevant. The postmodernist believes that we must create truth rather than discover it. The writings of the past such as the Bible are contaminated with a view or prejudice from that past that now render it undependable. Things have changed and truth has to change with the times.

Romans 1 predicts this evolution of truth. In verse 18, it says that men will "hold the truth in unrighteousness." Think about that: claiming to hold the truth but in unrighteousness. My little brain can't comprehend something being true but not right. And while they profess themselves to be wise, they become fools according to verse 22 because they *"changed the truth of God into a lie"* (verse 25). Just as culture amends the constitution and rewrites history to suit the twenty-first century man, so we must "go beyond foundationalism." If you go beyond, I think you are moving the ancient landmarks to do so.

This isn't new as we saw it earlier in the new-evangelical thinking of Harold Okenga in the 1940s. Fundamentalist Christians are too dogmatic. We must re-think our position; re-shape our theology; and open dialogue with the enemy of sound doctrine!

DESIGNER TRUTH IS EXPERIENTIAL TRUTH

Second Timothy 4:3 goes further: *"For the time will come when they will not endure sound doctrine; but after their own lusts…."*

Paul predicts that man will trust his own selfish lusts over God's sovereign love. *"In those days there was no king in Israel: every man did that which was right in his own eyes"* (Judges 21:25). There was no king, no authority, no leadership; everyone did their own thing and thought their own thing. *"There is a way which seemeth right unto a man, but the end thereof are the ways of death"* (Proverbs 14:12).

The postmodern man buys into Satan's lies today because of his sinful nature that does not want to come under the authority of God but rather live according to our fleshly lust. This is why many reject Jesus Christ as their Saviour. It's not that they don't want to go to heaven when they die—everybody wants to end up there. But man doesn't want to quit sinning! *"And this is the condemnation, that light is come into the world, and men loved darkness rather than light, because their deeds were evil. For every one that doeth evil hateth the light, neither cometh to the light, lest his deeds should be reproved"* (John 3:19–20).

This is the reason man scoffs at God and the Bible today. There is no such thing as an atheist. Everyone believes there is a God. People say to me: "I don't believe in God." To which I reply: "God doesn't believe you." That's fair, isn't it—atheists don't believe in God and God doesn't believe in atheists. That's what the Bible says: *"Because that which may be known of God is manifest in them; for God hath shewed it unto them. For the invisible things of him from the creation of the world are clearly seen, being understood by the things that are made, even his eternal power and Godhead; so that they are without excuse"* (Romans 1:19–20). God has revealed himself to every man. Every person understands that there is a God and that what that God says is true. Romans 2:15 says that God has written His law on our hearts and our conscience bears witness to that fact.

So, if man knows there is a God and that what God says is true, why does he scoff at it and reject the Truth? Peter tells us it is because of their sinful lusts. They choose to be willingly ignorant of Truth so that they don't have to quit sinning. *"Knowing this first, that there shall come in the last days scoffers, walking after their own lusts, And saying, Where is the promise of his coming? for since the fathers fell asleep, all things continue as they were from the beginning of the creation. For this they willingly are ignorant of, that by the word of God the heavens were of old, and the earth standing out of the water and in the water: Whereby the world that then was, being overflowed with water, perished: But the heavens and the earth, which are now, by the same word are kept in store, reserved unto fire against the day of judgment and perdition of ungodly men"* (2 Peter 3:3–7).

Man rejects the Truth that condemns his sin and tries to create a truth that will allow him to live according to his fleshly lusts in the twenty-first century. They create truth based on what works for them. This is nothing but plain old pragmatism. The seeker-sensitive movement (which now the very leaders and proponents of such have stated that it didn't work) was built on pragmatism. For over a decade we were told to build "Burger King churches." Go out into your community and survey people asking them what they want in a church. Then go back and build a ministry that allows people to have a church "their way." This brought about all kinds of changes in churches with the most noticeable being the introduction of two different services. A "traditional" service for the old folks that weren't quite ready for all these changes, and a "contemporary" service for those ready to "rock to Jesus."

DESIGNER TRUTH IS ECLECTIC TRUTH

"For the time will come when they will not endure sound doctrine; but after their own lusts shall they heap to themselves teachers…." Notice the plurality of leadership and authority that is now desired—"teachers." Promise Keeper rallies and home school rallies were held on Sundays in place of the local church with many voices leading instead of rallying people around the under-shepherd that God has placed in authority. A plurality of elders and a buffet of Bibles were found in churches that now craved an eclectic truth. James warns us about having "many masters."

The world has a plurality of gods, so why not create a plurality of truth. The end result is that if you have more than one authority for Truth, it's not too long before you become your own authority. That describes postmodernism in a nutshell and the ridiculous thinking we have today. If it's true for you, then it is as true as it needs to be and no one has a right to question what you have chosen as truth for yourself.

DESIGNER TRUTH IS ELEVATED TRUTH

"And they shall turn away their ears from the truth, and shall be turned unto fables" (2 Timothy 4:4). Today people believe they are enlightened if they tolerate everything and believe nothing. Political and religious leaders have perfected the art

of talking without saying anything. *"Folly is set in great dignity"* (Ecclesiastes 10:6A). *"Professing themselves to be wise, they became fools"* (Romans 1:22). We are convinced that we are smarter than God. Most politicians don't read the Bible or pray and if they do, they sure wouldn't be dumb enough to tell anyone. Preachers don't "preach the Word" but rather spend time in the pulpit explaining what it really means or the way it should be translated.

I have mentioned this verse earlier, but please meditate on its content carefully in light of our present state of affairs. *"For thou hast trusted in thy wickedness: thou hast said, None seeth me. Thy wisdom and thy knowledge, it hath perverted thee; and thou hast said in thine heart, I am, and none else beside me"* (Isaiah 47:10). Our own wickedness is calling the shots today and we think God doesn't notice. We have puffed ourselves up in our wisdom and knowledge but in reality we have perverted the Truth in the process. We claim to be enlightened and dare anyone to question or challenge us. There is only one "I am" and you and I are not Him!

While I have tried to point out some capital "T" Truth along the way of our exposure of small letter "t" truth, let's go back through 2 Timothy 4 and contrast this popular "designer" truth with "discovered" Truth.

DISCOVERED TRUTH IS ETERNAL TRUTH

Paul begins chapter 4 with, *"I charge thee therefore before God...."* Everything starts with God because everything was created by

God. *In the beginning God created…"* (Genesis 1:1A). *"Every good gift and every perfect gift is from above, and cometh down from the Father of lights…"* (James 1:17A). God was, is, and always will be. *"I am Alpha and Omega, the beginning and the end, the first and the last"* (Revelation 22:13).

God was before we were, is while we are, and will be after we leave. That more or less puts Him in charge! It would seem wise to believe and trust the Truth that comes from the only eternal being—God.

DISCOVERED TRUTH IS ESTABLISHED TRUTH

God declares that He does not change. What He was in the beginning, He still is now, and will always be forever. *"For I am the LORD, I change not"* (Malachi 3:6). *"Of old hast thou laid the foundation of the earth: and the heavens are the work of thy hands. They shall perish, but thou shalt endure: yea, all of them shall wax old like a garment; as a vesture shalt thou change them, and they shall be changed: But thou art the same, and thy years shall have no end"* (Psalm 102:25–27). Hebrews 13:8 declares, *"Jesus Christ the same yesterday, and to day, and for ever."*

Because God doesn't change, it would be a violation of His character to change His Word. God's Word does not evolve; it is not being created as we go; it is eternally established. Notice the ending to James 1:17: *"Every good gift and every perfect gift is from above, and cometh down from the Father of lights, with whom is no variableness, neither shadow of turning."* Numbers 23:19

is very clear about what God says: *"God is not a man, that he should lie; neither the son of man, that he should repent: hath he said, and shall he not do it? or hath he spoken, and shall he not make it good?"*

For example: let's take a man who in his finite and limited thinking decides that he would like marriage to be between two men. That suits his lusts and according to postmodernism we must tolerate his desires because we can't really know truth except through our own experience. This man's experience tells him that he gets great satisfaction out of this kind of relationship. No one should be allowed to condemn him for that would be a "hate crime." Laws must be passed to put him on equal footing with those who believe the contrary. The problem is that standing outside the circle of his finite and limited brain is a God who created him and has already established what the truth is in this matter. *"And the LORD God caused a deep sleep to fall upon Adam, and he slept: and he took one of his ribs, and closed up the flesh instead thereof; And the rib, which the LORD God had taken from man, made he a woman, and brought her unto the man. And Adam said, This is now bone of my bones, and flesh of my flesh: she shall be called Woman, because she was taken out of Man. Therefore shall a man leave his father and his mother, and shall cleave unto his wife: and they shall be one flesh"* (Genesis 2:21–24). *"Thou shalt not lie with mankind, as with womankind: it is abomination"* (Leviticus 18:22).

That thinking isn't popular, in vogue, trendy, or fashionable. But it is the Truth. By the way, we're all sinners and everything that is contrary to the Truth that God has established is sin. *"All unrighteousness is sin"* (1 John 5:17A). But God forgives sin! All sin! Any sin! God balances Truth with His love and while the Truth condemns all of us as sinners, His love is able to save us from that sin and bring us back into fellowship with Him. I don't see that as a hate crime. *"Know ye not that the unrighteous shall not inherit the kingdom of God? Be not deceived: neither fornicators, nor idolaters, nor adulterers, nor effeminate, nor abusers of themselves with mankind, Nor thieves, nor covetous, nor drunkards, nor revilers, nor extortioners, shall inherit the kingdom of God. And such were some of you: but ye are washed, but ye are sanctified, but ye are justified in the name of the Lord Jesus, and by the Spirit of our God"* (1 Corinthians 6:9–11). God defines sin; hates that sin; but is willing to forgive sin—that's worth celebrating, not criminalizing.

Paul doesn't exhort Timothy to live by his experience or what he thinks is best, but by the doctrine he mentions in 2 Timothy 4:2 and the "sound doctrine" he mentions in verse 3. In his ministry, he simply says: *"Preach the word"* (2 Timothy 4:2).

DISCOVERED TRUTH IS EXAMINING TRUTH

It is time to stop reading our Bibles! We are in desperate need to let the Bible read us. We have too many Bible studies and not enough of the Bible studying us. Paul tells Timothy to live by and preach the Word of God because it "reproves," "rebukes," and "exhorts." Jeremiah 17:9 reminds us that *"The heart is deceitful above all things, and desperately wicked: who can know it?"* But *"…the word of God is quick, and powerful, and sharper* than any twoedged sword, piercing even to the dividing asunder of soul and spirit, and of the joints and marrow, and is a discerner of the thoughts and intents of the heart"* (Hebrews 4:12). We are blind to our hearts' conditions, but the Truth of God's Word reveals and brings to light the hidden things that are there.

While the eclectic designers examine their buffet of Bibles in their seminary cloisters, we need a generation of people who will let the absolute Truth of God's Word examine them! Too many people today look at the Bible as the "object." We are the "subject" and we spend all of our time studying the "object." It is time to reverse the process. We need to become the "object" and let the "subject"—God's Word—study us. We have classes on how to study the Bible but few today are willing to go to class and let the Bible study them. How desperately today we need the examination of Truth.

DISCOVERED TRUTH IS ENDURING TRUTH

In 2 Timothy 4:5, Paul turns his attention on Timothy and tells him, *"But watch thou in all things, endure afflictions, do the work of an evangelist, make full proof of thy ministry."* He is telling Timothy to stay by the stuff. Don't quit! It was going to get tough for Timothy, and no doubt, after his mentor had passed off the scene, he would be tempted to give up. But Paul reminds him that he must endure, because his message endures. We must finish our course because God's Word always accomplishes that which it is sent to do.

The bull's eye is Truth because it is the Truth that changes lives. I was sitting in the pastor's car on a beautiful fall afternoon in Wisconsin. We had been out soulwinning and had stopped by the church to pick up his children from the Christian school. As we pulled into the parking lot, he informed me that it would be a few minutes before school was out and so he was going to quickly run into his office to check on any messages. He informed me that I could wait in the car or come in with him. I opted for the car because it was a beautiful day, and I wanted to enjoy it for a few minutes.

Soon other parents drove in and parked to wait for their children. A lady parked nearby and got out and came over to the window on the passenger side of the car where I was seated. My window was already down and so we quickly exchanged greetings. She then lifted a large brown paper bag through the window and into my lap and said: "This is for you." I said, "Thanks," and she returned to her car.

I opened the bag and discovered a plastic five quart ice cream pail filled with freshly baked, homemade, right out of the oven, chocolate chip cookies! A whole pail full of them! I pulled back the lid on that pail and the aroma of those cookies filled the car. I picked one up and it broke in my hand. The chocolate, still warm, was dripping down into the pail! One bite and I was addicted! After devouring three or four, I began to slow down a bit and noticed that there was something under the pail.

Between bites I lifted the pail and set it on the car seat beside me and investigated the rest of the contents of the bag. On the bottom was a beautifully wrapped present with a white ribbon and bow. Underneath the ribbon was a card with my name on the outside. I lifted it from the bag and looked at it curiously. Why would anyone buy me a present? It wasn't my birthday or any special occasion.

I don't know how you are with presents and cards, but I like presents better than cards. Cards are great, but if there is a present with the card, I am far more interested in the present. I took the card off of the package and threw it on the seat next to the pail of cookies and proceeded to rip into the package. Off came the bow and ribbon, then the paper, and finally the tape that held the lid. As I pushed back the lid and pulled off some tissue paper, I saw it! There inside that box was a brand new, no scratches on it, right from the store, "hammer head." The top of a hammer that you pound nails with. It was brand new. The wooden handle of the hammer was also new but it was broken off about three inches from the hammer's head. There was a brand new hammer with a broken handle.

I thought, "What kind of a cruel joke is this?" Then I remembered the card! When all else fails, read the directions, dummy. I opened that card and this is what it said: "Dear Dr. Goetsch, All week long I have been listening to you preach the Bible. I have sat in my seat and argued with every point. I convinced myself that what you were saying was just your interpretation and opinion. But as you can see the Bible which is represented by the hammer's head has come out of the argument without a scratch. (It always does.) But the handle, which represents my will has been broken. Early this morning, around 2:30, by the side of my bed, I finally got on my knees and submitted my life to the Truth."

I looked at that "piece of junk" in that box, bowed my head and thanked God for such a wonderful reminder of how my life needed to be—broken and submissive to the Truth of God's Word. That's why Satan has put the Truth in the bull's eye. Truth is the target. If Satan can destroy Truth, people will be destroyed with it—for eternity.

SIX

THE TACTIC
A BREACH OF SECURITY

*Beware of false prophets, which come to you
in sheep's clothing, but inwardly they are
ravening wolves.*—MATTHEW 7:15

"Remove your shoes, jackets and sweaters. All liquids, jells, and pastes must be in a plastic bag. Computers and electronic devices must be placed in a bin." The sights and sounds of a security checkpoint at the airport are all too familiar since 9/11. We have become very aware of the fact that we are susceptible to attack since the bombing of the World Trade Center by the infiltration of our borders by terrorists. As we drive along the southwest portion of our nation, we are aware that our vehicle may be checked by border patrol with trained dogs looking for illegal immigrants, drugs, or weapons.

Infiltration is a concern, but not just in the area of national security. We are careful about what we eat and drink, we wash our hands, and are conscious of the air we breathe lest some virus or germ infiltrate our body. We spend money on security systems to protect our vehicles, homes, and personal identity. We memorize our personal identification numbers or at best keep them hidden so as not to have our bank account or credit card emptied unexpectedly. Any breach of our security is a major concern, and we take all of the precautions available to protect ourselves.

We must be no less vigilant with the Truth. In Matthew 7:15, Jesus warns: *"Beware of false prophets, which come to you in sheep's clothing, but inwardly they are ravening wolves."* Notice, they will come to us disguised in some way in order to infiltrate. We saw earlier in Matthew 23 how the Pharisees were described by Christ as whited sepulchers which on the outside appeared to be religious and pious, but inwardly were full of hypocrisy and iniquity. Infiltration is one of Satan's oldest tricks.

Infiltration was the purpose for the short little epistle of Jude. *"Beloved, when I gave all diligence to write unto you of the common salvation, it was needful for me to write unto you, and exhort you that ye should earnestly contend for the faith which was once delivered unto the saints. For there are certain men crept in unawares, who were before of old ordained to this condemnation, ungodly men, turning the grace of our God into lasciviousness, and denying the only Lord God, and our Lord Jesus Christ"* (Jude 2–3). Later the language becomes more graphic as the security alert is turned up warning us of the danger of such an invasion. *"These are spots in your feasts of charity, when they feast with you, feeding themselves without fear: clouds they are without water, carried about of winds: trees whose fruit withereth, without fruit, twice dead, plucked up by the roots; Raging waves of the sea, foaming out their own shame; wandering stars, to whom is reserved the blackness of darkness for ever"* (Jude 12–13). The word *spots* in verse 12 carries the connotation of a reef beneath the surface of the water. It is often not visible to the naked eye, but can rip the ship apart and cause great loss of property and life.

Why would the Bible carry warnings about such activity? Surely the first century church would not face this kind of threat. The early church saw tremendous growth and the persecution that came only caused more growth. Surely Satan would not be able to infiltrate such a powerful movement. The Bible indicates otherwise. In fact, infiltration started when the church started. Jesus chose twelve disciples and one of them was a devil. *"Jesus answered them, Have not I chosen you twelve, and one of you is a devil? He spake of Judas Iscariot the son of Simon: for he it was that should betray him, being one of the twelve"* (John 6:70–71).

Judas was so good in his disguise that even when Jesus exposed him, the other disciples didn't suspect him. *"When Jesus had thus said, he was troubled in spirit, and testified, and said, Verily, verily, I say unto you, that one of you shall betray me. Then the disciples looked one on another, doubting of whom he spake. Now there was leaning on Jesus' bosom one of his disciples, whom Jesus loved. Simon Peter therefore beckoned to him, that he should ask who it should be of whom he spake. He then lying on Jesus' breast saith unto him, Lord, who is it? Jesus answered, He it is, to whom I shall give a sop, when I have dipped it. And when he had dipped the sop, he gave it to Judas Isacriot, the son of Simon. And after the sop Satan entered into him. Then said Jesus unto him, That thou doest, do quickly. Now no man at the table knew for what intent he spake*

INFILTRATION IS ONE OF SATAN'S OLDEST TRICKS.

this unto him. For some of them thought, because Judas had the bag, that Jesus had said unto him, Buy those things that we have need of against the feast; or, that he should give something to the poor. He then having received the sop went immediately out: and it was night" (John 13:21–30). I have a hunch that Judas was a good preacher. I know he was trusted by the other disciples because he kept their money. The Bible indicates that he performed miracles right along with the other disciples. He had infiltrated the ranks undetected.

The Apostle Paul was aware of infiltration in the church at Thessalonica. A rumor or perhaps a letter supposedly written by the Apostle, was circulating that Jesus had already returned. Thus Paul writes in chapter 2: *"Now we beseech you, brethren, by the coming of our Lord Jesus Christ, and by our gathering together unto him, That ye be not soon shaken in mind, or be troubled, neither by spirit, nor by word, nor by letter as from us, as that the day of Christ is at hand. Let no man deceive you by any means"* (2 Thessalonians 2:1–3A). This false message had appeared authentic and had all of the markings of truth, but in reality it was the infiltration of a lie.

ERROR DOESN'T LOOK LIKE ERROR; IT LOOKS LIKE TRUTH.

Many of us have memorized 2 Timothy 2:15: *"Study to shew thyself approved unto God, a workman that needeth not to be ashamed, rightly dividing the word of truth."* But why did Paul emphasize the study of Truth to young Timothy? Read on: *"But shun profane and vain babblings: for they will increase unto more ungodliness. And their word will eat as doth a canker: of whom is Hymenaeus and Philetus; Who concerning the truth have erred, saying that the resurrection is past already; and overthrown the faith of some"* (2 Timothy 2:16–18). Security had already been breached and the Truth was at risk. Paul needed this young preacher to be schooled rigorously in the Scriptures so that he would be able to detect the error.

> STUDYING THE GENUINE WILL ENABLE US TO SPOT THE COUNTERFEITS.

The Apostle John was concerned about the damage that one of the members was causing in the church when he wrote in 3 John 9: *"I wrote unto the church: but Diotrephes, who loveth to have the preeminence among them, receiveth us not."* He later commends Demetrius to them saying that this man *"hath good report of all men, and of the truth itself"* (3 John 12A). The Truth was indeed under attack from within. Infiltration has been Satan's tactic from the beginning.

But how does error slip in unnoticed? Well remember, Satan doesn't act like Satan, he acts like God. Error doesn't look like error; it looks like Truth. The early church was dealing with Gnosticism which was a blending of Christian doctrine and symbolism with worldly philosophies. Clothed in Christian imagery and terminology, these errors fooled a lot of God's people. Many of the cults of our day borrow Bible terminology but redefine the terms and reconstruct the doctrine. Gnosticism always parades itself as more enlightened than everyone else with access to knowledge that no one else possesses. Gnosticism is always mutating like a modern day flu virus spawning new errors that are difficult to pinpoint and eliminate.

The "Gospel of Thomas" and "The Gospel of Judas" were some early forms of this mixture of error with Truth. In more recent days we have dealt with "The Passion," "The Da Vinci Code," and the movie "2012." Amazingly even Christians know more about what is in these books and on these movies than they know from the Bible and thus the danger. John writes in 2 John 10–11, *"If there come any unto you, and bring not this doctrine, receive him not into your house, neither bid him God speed. For he that biddeth him God speed is partaker of his evil deeds."* Sadly, many of God's people do not know their Bibles well enough to know that much of what is infiltrating our churches today is not biblical truth and are welcoming it with open arms. In some cases, Satan doesn't have to infiltrate our churches; the pastor and people are going to the conferences, reading the books, and subscribing to the blogs of those teaching the error.

At graduation each year of the college I attended, the president of the school, Dr. B. Myron Cedarholm would choose a verse or two for each graduate. As their name was called to walk across the platform they would proceed to the podium, stop, and he would read the verse to them that he had selected. It was painfully slow and as a freshman, sophomore, and junior, I thought it was the dumbest thing I had ever seen. Commencement would last well past four hours and it was outside in the hot June sun!

However, when my name was called on June 1, 1974, and I walked across that platform and stopped by the side of my mentor, with humble thanksgiving, I received the verses he had selected for me. I know that God had to have led him to the selection because at that time no one in that audience would have thought of me as a preacher. (I had only preached three times in my life at that point.) I have pondered the verses often since that day, but numerous times in recent days. They are one of the major reasons I decided to preach on this subject and write this book. He read for me Titus 1:9–11: *"Holding fast the faithful word as he hath been taught, that he may be able by sound doctrine both to exhort and to convince the gainsayers. For there are many unruly and vain talkers and deceivers, specially they of the circumcision: Whose mouths must be stopped, who subvert whole houses, teaching things which they ought not, for filthy lucre's sake."*

Truth is under attack and no doubt the terrorists who seek to destroy it have infiltrated our ranks just as they have in the past. The problem is real; the stakes are high; the time is short; and the outcome is eternal. So what do we do? Do we quit? Let's go back "to the law and to the testimony." The book of Jude after warning us that some have "crept in unawares" gives this advice: *"But, beloved, remember ye the words which were spoken before of the apostles of our Lord Jesus Christ; How that they told you there should be mockers in the last time, who should walk after their own ungodly lusts. These be they who separate themselves, sensual, having not the spirit"* (Jude 17–19). Remember the words which have been spoken. Go back to Truth. We don't need to study the counterfeit; we need to study the Truth. Doing so will enable us to spot the counterfeit.

In the closing verses of Jude, God gives us five directives as we study and obey the Truth. As we place these disciplines into our daily lives, we can impact this world in spite of Satan's attack.

DON'T STOP BUILDING

But ye, beloved, building up yourselves….—JUDE 20

Those who love and defend the Truth are going to have to stay healthy. The hour calls for us to "be strong in the Lord." This is no time for anorexic and bulimic Christians. We have a war to fight! *"Ye therefore, beloved, seeing ye know these things before, beware lest ye also, being led away with the error of the wicked, fall from your own stedfastness. But grow in grace, and in the knowledge of our Lord and Saviour Jesus Christ. To him be glory both now and for ever. Amen"* (2 Peter 3:17–18).

Discernment between Truth and error is impossible without a healthy diet in God's Word. *"But strong meat belongeth to them that are of full age, even those who by reason of use have their senses exercised to discern both good and evil"* (Hebrews 5:14). Peter adds: *"Whereby are given unto us exceeding great and precious promises: that by these ye might be partakers of the divine nature, having escaped the corruption that is in the world through lust"* (2 Peter 1:4). Mature discipleship is only developed through a saturation of the life with Truth. *"If ye continue in my word, then are ye my disciples indeed"* (John 8:31B).

WE ARE JUSTIFIED BY FAITH AND WE MUST NOW JOURNEY BY FAITH.

In the high desert where we live, we can get some pretty strong wind. Coming from the Midwest, it took awhile for me to get used to this daily weather activity. I noticed early on that when anyone planted a tree, they always staked it with two or three posts around it to keep it straight. The older and larger trees have to be "thinned" every couple of years so that the wind can blow through them instead of blowing them over!

One day as I was pulling out of my driveway, I noticed that one of our trees in the yard had blown over. I didn't have time to do much about it and fortunately it wasn't in anyone's way, so I drove to the campus and later phoned my wife to make some plans as to what to do. By that time, a man had stopped by and inquired if he could have the wood. I went home, met him, and arranged for him to clean everything up in return for the wood. I was concerned that he would saw the trunk off as close to the ground as possible so that we would not have an ugly stump in the yard. As we walked over to the base of that tree, we were both shocked. I had never seen anything like it in my life. The tree had sheered off right at the surface of the ground and there were literally no roots. We pulled on the few pieces of wood that remained out of the ground with our bare hands. That tree went down because while it had some growth on the surface, it never went deep into the earth where the nourishment and water for growth could be found. When the winds blew, it fell!

When God instituted the local church, He provided men to that church that could teach us Truth. The winds are going to blow, and the wise Christian sinks his roots down deep in the preaching and teaching of God's Word so that he can withstand the storm. *"And he gave some, apostles; and some, prophets; and some, evangelists; and some, pastors and teachers; For the perfecting of the saints, for the work of the ministry, for the edifying of the body of Christ: Till we all come in the unity of the faith, and of the knowledge of the Son of God, unto a perfect man, unto the measure of the stature of the fullness of Christ: That we henceforth be no more children, tossed to and fro, and carried about with every wind of doctrine, by the sleight of men, and cunning craftiness, whereby they lie in wait to deceive; But speaking the truth in love, may grow up into him in all things, which is the head, even Christ: From whom the whole body fitly joined together and compacted by that which every joint supplieth, according to the effectual working in the measure of every part, maketh increase of the body unto the edifying of itself in love"* (Ephesians 4:11–16). Don't stop building your life!

DON'T STOP BELIEVING

But ye, beloved, building up yourselves on your most holy faith....—JUDE 20

We are justified by faith and we must now journey by faith. *"Behold, his soul which is lifted up is not upright in him: but the just shall live by his faith"* (Habakkuk 2:4). We won't make it on our own and in our own strength. We must have faith! *"Believe in the LORD your God, so shall ye be established"* (2 Chronicles 20:20B). Satan is aiming his darts so, *"Above all, taking the shield of faith, wherewith ye shall be able to quench all the fiery darts of the wicked"* (Ephesians 6:16).

God doesn't need great numbers, He needs great faith within that number. Jonathan and his armour bearer found themselves surrounded by natural barriers and a garrison of Philistines. There were but two of them and a whole host of the enemy. Humanly speaking, they were sunk. *"And Jonathan said to the young man that bare his armour, Come, and let us go over unto the garrison of these uncircumcised: it may be that the* LORD *will work for us: for there is no restraint to the* LORD *to save by many or by few"* (1 Samuel 14:6). God honored the faith of Jonathan and the enemy was defeated as God miraculously intervened.

David didn't fear Goliath because he had seen God work before, and so by faith he confidently went to battle. *"David said moreover, The* LORD *that delivered me out of the paw of the lion, and out of the paw of the bear, he will deliver me out of the hand of this Philistine"* (1 Samuel 17:37A). Our Goliath grows taller each day or so it seems, and often we are at a loss as to what we should do. Jehoshaphat found himself in that predicament. *"O our God, wilt thou not judge them? for we have no might against this great company that cometh against us; neither know we what to do: but our eyes are upon thee"* (2 Chronicles 20:12). Where are our eyes? If we fix our eyes on the enemy of Truth we will never leave camp, but if we focus our eyes on God, we will confidently attack.

In a sense, it does seem like the whole world is against the Truth. Satan seems to control everything and all of his guns are loaded and aimed at Truth. I found myself frustrated after a recent election. It didn't go exactly like I had hoped and prayed that it would. The next morning I was reading Hebrews 11, and I came to verse 33: *"Who through faith subdued kingdoms...."* My jaw dropped as I pondered those words. Kingdoms stacked against God's people and yet they were subdued—by faith. Don't stop believing. Pray with the apostles of old: *"Lord, Increase our faith"* (Luke 17:5B).

PRAYER IS NOT THE LEAST WE CAN DO, BUT THE MOST WE CAN DO.

DON'T STOP BEGGING

...praying in the Holy Ghost.—Jude 20

Prayer connects our poverty to His power. God says we don't have because we don't ask. Too often we wait until all of our resources are exhausted before we pray. We look at prayer as a last resort. During an invitation in St. Paul, Minnesota one night as a young preacher, I said: "If you have a need, I would like to pray for you. If you will lift your hand, I will see it and have prayer. It's the least I can do for you." Later, at the back of the church, a sweet but determined older lady marched up to me and emphatically informed me that prayer was not the "least" I could do for her, but the "most" I could do for her. What a powerful truth!

"The effectual fervent prayer of a righteous man availeth much" (James 5:16B). *"And he spake a parable unto them to this end, that men ought always to pray, and not to faint"* (Luke 18:1). *"Seek the LORD and his strength, seek his face continually"* (1 Chronicles 16:11). We don't have to hesitate or be timid about prayer. God commands us to *"...come boldly unto the throne of grace, that we may obtain mercy, and find grace to help in time of need"* (Hebrews 4:16).

God wants to answer prayer! One summer I had been out on the road in revival meetings but was scheduled to come back home to preach the Sunday services at Lancaster Baptist Church. I would be in and back out in about thirty-six hours. Dr. Rasmussen, the vice president of the college called me the day before I flew in and said: "Brother Goetsch, we have about thirty seniors on our prospect list for college who are trying to decide about coming to school this fall. We have been calling them and writing them, but I thought that it might encourage them if you could jot them a note on a postcard and send it to them." I agreed that it was a good idea and asked him if he could secure the postcards for me and address them, so that when I arrived home I could quickly do them or take them on the road with me when I left.

I had time to slip by my office on Saturday night when I arrived to pick up my mail and check on a few things before the services the next day. There on the corner of my desk, as promised, were those thirty postcards. They were neatly addressed and stamped, ready for me to take it from there. I had a few minutes so I decided to sit down right then and do them. It took about an hour, but I finished the task and placed them on the corner of my secretary's desk with a note asking her to mail them out Monday morning.

After the Sunday evening service, Peter Mordh, our director of recruitment, came up to me in the lobby of the church rather nervously. He said, "Brother Goetsch, I know you are extremely busy and you are going to be leaving again in the morning, but I was wondering if you could do us a favor? We have about thirty seniors who…." I put up my hand in the middle of his request and said, "Peter, it's already done!" He said, "What?" I stated, "What you were going to ask me. It's already done." "What do you mean?" he quizzically and confusedly inquired. I said, "The postcards to the thirty seniors. They are already written and ready to send out in the morning. They are on my secretary's desk." Dumbfounded, he said, "How did you know?" Without cracking a smile I said, "Brother Mordh, it says in Isaiah 65:24,

'And it shall come to pass, that before they call, I will answer; and while they are yet speaking, I will hear.'"

He shook his head and walked away totally confused. I have laughed about that many times since. (I'm not sure I ever told Peter about my connection to his request through Dr. Rasmussen). I'm not omniscient, but God is, and what a powerful truth, that before we can pray, He is already delivering the answer. Don't stop begging!

DON'T STOP BULWARKING

Keep yourselves in the love of God, looking for the mercy of our Lord Jesus Christ unto eternal life.—JUDE 21

Guarding our own heart is a full-time job and a difficult one. The word *heart* is found over eight-hundred times in Scripture. The devil knows that if he can penetrate our heart, he's got our life for *"as he thinketh in his heart, so is he"* (Proverbs 23:7A). Earlier in Proverbs 4:23, Solomon exhorts his son to *"Keep thy heart with all diligence; for out of it are the issues of life."*

There is a very interesting verse in Ecclesiastes 10:2. It says: *"A wise man's heart is at his right hand; but a fool's heart at his left."* I don't believe that God is trashing left-handed people here. All of us have a dominant hand and a weak hand. The majority of people, by quite a large percentage, are right-handed. Their right hand is their strong hand and their left is their weak hand. Now God says, that a wise man will keep his heart in his strong hand while a fool holds it in his weak hand.

I started playing football in seventh grade and enjoyed playing all the way through college. In those ten years, they never let me touch the ball. I was not what they call a "skill" player. It wasn't that I wouldn't have liked to play running back or receiver, but farm boys like me normally don't possess those "pretty boy" skills. We generally end up in the trenches, where the game is won or lost, I might add!

Hanging out on the football field for ten years however, I did observe the time and energy that went into protecting the ball. The quarterbacks and centers would come out thirty minutes before the rest of the players were required to be on the field and just work on the snap or hiking of the ball from the center to the quarterback. When we used a shotgun formation, it was even more crucial that they spent that time practicing the initial exchange of the play. As we were over on one side of the field hitting blocking sleds and banging ourselves into tackling dummies, the coaches across the way would be screaming at those skill players to "PROTECT THE BALL!" They would work for hours on the handoff from the quarterback to the running back. Receivers were drilled until they were numb on looking the ball into their hands and then tucking it away once it was caught.

No player was allowed to "flaunt" or "hot-dog it" with the ball. If you had the ball, you were to keep it close to your body with one hand over one end and the other end of that ball tightly tucked into the crux of your elbow. When a tackler would approach, they would cover the ball with their other hand. Why? Because guys like me were over on the other side of the field, working for hours developing skills to jerk the ball loose!

When making a tackle we would practice stripping the ball by coming down over the top of it or punching it loose by bringing our fist under the ball carriers arm.

Turnovers are the difference between winning and losing. Too many Christians have their heart in their left hand. We are careless and indifferent about the skill of our enemy to steal it away from God. We must keep our heart with diligence if we expect to win this battle. Many ministries today have lost their "heart." They go through motions and maintain status quo, but there is no heart for God and for Truth. The enemy has stripped many a church and school of their heart and the battle was lost.

Robert Murray McCheyne soberly reminds us of the importance of "keeping" our heart and life: "How diligently the cavalry officer keeps his saber clean and sharp; every stain he rubs off with the greatest of care. Remember, you are God's instrument. I trust, a chosen vessel unto Him to bear His name. In great measure, according to the purity and perfection of the instrument, will be the success. It is not great talents God blesses so much as likeness to Jesus. A holy minister is an awful weapon in the hand of God."

Don't stop bulwarking! The defense and propagation of Truth depends on it.

DON'T STOP BECKONING

And of some have compassion, making a difference; And others save with fear, pulling them out of the fire; hating even the garment spotted by the flesh.—JUDE 22–23

We can't allow ourselves to get so frustrated with the weeds that we stop growing wheat! A wicked attitude is developing rapidly across the landscape of our churches and schools. Many are coming to the conclusion that not everyone "can" be saved. I honestly believe that many are embracing a theology out of apathy rather than conviction. John 3:16 says that God loves the world. Second Corinthians 5:15 declares that Jesus Christ died for all!

I've listened to the arguments and read the articles, and maybe I'm not as enlightened as scholars in the seats of higher criticism, but I can't trample on the Truth of 2 Peter 3:9: *"The Lord is not slack concerning his promise, as some men count slackness; but is longsuffering to us-ward, not willing that any should perish, but that all should come to repentance."* I'm not smart enough to be able to explain away 1 Timothy 2:3–4 where it says: *"For this is good and acceptable in the sight of God our Saviour; Who will have all men to be saved, and to come unto the knowledge of the truth."*

I'm sure someone will write a book to refute this one, but before you buy that one, could I plead with you to keep on winning souls to Christ? Let's continue to plant churches and preach the Gospel. We must send and support missionaries around the world. Don't stop giving invitations, and keep the baptistry filled with water. Develop a discipleship program and teach others to do the same. God commands it: *"And the things that thou hast heard of me among many witnesses, the same commit thou to faithful men, who shall be able to teach others also"* (2 Timothy 2:2). God promises to give the results if we will keep on keeping on. *"And let us not be weary in well doing: for in due season we shall reap, if we faint not"* (Galatians 6:9).

Some time ago, a pastor called and asked if I would come and preach for his church's thirtieth anniversary. I had preached for him a few times previously and always enjoyed his fellowship and good liberty to preach among his people. We set the date, and I began to pray that God would allow me to be a blessing.

As the time approached, he wrote and said that they were going to attempt to knock on every door in their town in preparation for this anniversary. The church was not that large and the town was a difficult field to say the least. I decided to try to get there in time to help with some door knocking on Saturday. I enjoyed going out with that pastor and his people. By the end of the day, every door in that community had received an invitation to come to the services on the following morning and afternoon. This good pastor and people were tired from a busy week but eagerly anticipated a wonderful day.

I taught Sunday school the next morning to the regular crowd of members and dismissed a little early so that we could have time to greet our visitors that would come in for the morning service. We were ready to greet, but none came. I noticed the pastor waited until about five minutes after the hour to start the service. I'm sure that he was sure somebody would show up! No one did. He tried to keep a "stiff upper lip" as they say, and lead the service with enthusiasm but his disappointment was obvious. For thirty years he had labored in this town faithfully, had raised a godly family, and now just wanted to see God do something great for His glory.

They had a dinner on the grounds, and I enjoyed the meal with the members of the church. Everyone tried to be happy and rejoice as best we could. We were scheduled to have an afternoon service at 2:00 PM so that folks could eat, attend the service and then return home. After finishing my meal, I decided to leave the table and go into the auditorium where I had left my Bible and go over my notes for the afternoon service. I was burdened to somehow try to be a blessing to this discouraged pastor and people who had worked so hard.

When I stepped into the auditorium, a lady was sitting about two rows from the back that I did not recognize from the morning service. I went and greeted her and found that she was a visitor who had come for the afternoon service. After a little small talk, I excused myself and quickly went to find the pastor. I informed him of our visitor and he and his wife came inside and conversed with her briefly before the service. By the time we started, seven first-time visitors had made their way into the auditorium. I opted for a Gospel message in place of my "God will reward you in heaven" one.

When I gave the invitation, several of those visitors walked the aisle for salvation. Tears flowed as people rejoiced in God's faithfulness. I was standing in the little hallway at the back of the church, when the pastor's wife emerged from the counseling room with the visiting lady who had first entered the church that afternoon. She took the pastor's hand and said: "Pastor, you probably don't remember me, but you knocked on my door thirty years ago. I remember it plainly. You told me you were new in town and starting a Baptist church. I thought you were crazy and never gave a thought to ever attending.

"This week, someone stopped by my house and left the flyer for the anniversary Sunday. I couldn't believe it had been thirty years. When I saw your picture on the flyer, I thought to myself, that man invited me thirty years ago; I believe I will go. I came and I found Christ as my Saviour!" Now we were all crying! But they were tears of joy; *"They that sow in tears shall reap in joy. He that goeth forth and weepeth, bearing precious seed, shall doubtless come again with rejoicing, bringing his sheaves with him"* (Psalm 126:5–6). Don't stop beckoning!

The Transportation Security Association and the Border Patrol will never be able to completely stop infiltration of terrorists into our country. Somewhere along the line, someone will slip through with an intent to destroy. Likewise, no matter how vigilant we try to be, Satan is a whole lot smarter than we are and has many more resources at his disposal. But our God is greater than our enemy, and if we will be faithful we can grow some wheat in spite of his sowing of weeds.

If I see a weed, I believe that I have a responsibility to pull it out. But I must stay focused on the harvest. Listen to the advice Jesus gave to His disciples: *"Another parable put he forth unto them, saying, The kingdom of heaven is likened unto a man which sowed good seed in his field: But while men slept, his enemy came and sowed tares among the wheat, and went his way. But when the blade was sprung up, and brought forth fruit, then appeared the tares also. So the servants of the householder came and said unto him, Sir, didst not thou sow good seed in thy field? from whence then hath it tares? He said unto them, An enemy hath done this. The servants said unto him, Wilt thou then that we go and gather them up? But he said, Nay; lest while ye gather up the tares, ye root up also the wheat with them. Let both grow together until the harvest: and in the time of harvest I will say to the reapers, Gather ye together first the tares, and bind them in bundles to burn them: but gather the wheat into my barn"* (Matthew 13:24–30).

Keep sowing—God will do the sorting!

SEVEN

THE TEST
CHAMPIONS OR CHAMELEONS

But Daniel purposed in his heart that he would not defile himself with the portion of the king's meat, nor with the wine which he drank: therefore he requested of the prince of the eunuchs that he might not defile himself.—DANIEL 1:8

When I was a boy, we lived in the country and had a "party line" telephone. When I mention a "party line" telephone to teenagers today, they think, "Cool!" No! It was not cool. A party line telephone meant, at least in our case, that you shared a phone number with seven of your neighbors. Eight families all had the same telephone number. When the phone rang, eight people said, "Hello." After you determined who the phone call was for—no one hung up—they all continued to listen to "your" conversation! For entertainment back in those days, we didn't watch television or listen to the radio, we picked up the phone.

The telephone has certainly evolved in my lifetime. Today, it seems that a cell phone is included in the gift bag of necessary items they send home with your baby from the hospital. The smallest of children are carrying cell phones. And our phones have become more than talking devices—they are cameras, video recorders, GPS, mini-internet systems, etc. They are our connection to the world and we have come to depend on them.

The phone is just one of many examples of rapid changes that are taking place in our world. But it is not just technology that is fueling change. The world is changing the way it thinks. God and the Bible—Truth—is not a part of our thinking today. Secular humanism has encouraged man to become his own god. We worship the earth but not the eternal One who created all. *"Who changed the truth of God into a lie, and worshipped and served the creature more than the Creator, who is blessed for ever. Amen"* (Romans 1:25).

I marvel at just how fast all of this change is taking place. I can remember when the principal of my public elementary school would pray over the intercom system at the start of each school day. I can recall the days when stores and restaurants were closed for business on Sunday. There was a day in my lifetime where it was illegal to swear on television or show a bedroom scene even if no one was in the bed! When I went to college I did not know what a homosexual was and had no concept of a gang or graffiti. I had never heard of any other Bible other than the King James Version, and I had no concept of a "para-church" organization. Women preachers were unheard of and rap music hadn't been invented so no one was rapping the Gospel. Christians didn't go to the movies or the beach, didn't socially drink, and believed marriage vows to be sacred. Preachers wore ties, preached from pulpits, and actually lived holy lives.

I could go on and on about change, but the point is the acceleration of the change. We aren't walking away from God—we're running from Him. We must understand the principle that every step away from God gets doubled. We comprehend this principle from the other side of the coin. *"Draw nigh to God, and he will draw nigh to you"* (James 4:8). When you take a step toward God, He moves a step toward you. Every step you take toward Him gets doubled, because He is moving toward you with each step. The reverse is likewise true.

When we move away from God, He moves away from us. It's not that He loves the world any less today than He ever has or is less concerned in His love to mankind, but the distance is widening between God and man because of our rejection of Him. *"The LORD is with you, while ye be with him; and if ye seek him, he will be found of you; but if ye forsake him, he will forsake you"* (2 Chronicles 15:2b). We may not think we are moving that far, but the distance doubles with every move. One step becomes a series of changes—a walk becomes a run—and so on. Thus, changes that seem small and incidental leave gaps that become canyons between God and man. And we are left to wonder how it all happened so fast.

> WE MUST UNDERSTAND THAT EVERY STEP AWAY FROM GOD GETS DOUBLED.

Today, we look at the world, our nation, churches, and people and wonder how we will ever find our way back to God, if ever. In many ways we seem so far removed. We question whether revival is even possible and doubt that much of the world could get saved. But we must not lose hope. God requires us to be faithful no matter what is taking place around us. *"Therefore, my beloved brethren, be ye stedfast, unmoveable, always abounding in the work of the Lord, forasmuch as ye know that your labour is not in vain in the Lord"* (1 Corinthians 15:58). God predicts trouble, testing, and triumph in Revelation 2:10: *"Fear none of those things which thou shalt suffer: behold, the devil shall cast some of you into prison, that ye may be tried; and ye shall have tribulation ten days: be thou faithful unto death, and I will give thee a crown of life."*

How can we stay faithful and ultimately triumph in changing times? Our test has come just as it has to generations before us. The Bible gives us principles but also shows us people. He does so to encourage us to follow their example. *"Now all these things happened unto them for ensamples: and they are written for our admonition, upon whom the ends of the world are come"* (1 Corinthians 10:11). God has a way of using devastating changes to produce dynamic champions. Follow with me the steps of a champion in the midst of change.

AN END OF REVIVAL

There are two human characters in Scripture from whose lives the Holy Spirit chooses to record their relationship with God without exposing any flaws. We know they had them, for no one is perfect and sinless except our Saviour. These two characters are Joseph and Daniel. Interestingly, both of these men lived during times of tumultuous change, yet they remained steadfast and unmovable. They were forced to live in pagan cultures and tempted to compromise the Truth they knew, but both refused. Their testimonies reveal the thrilling events and divine intervention of a holy God. As they refused to compromise, each conflict developed them into more of the champion God desired. Both were used by God to lead and deliver their people. The changes of the twenty-first century can develop modern day champions for "such a time as this." Let's focus on one of these champions from the Old Testament.

As chapter 1 of Daniel opens, we immediately notice **A Departure**. *"In the third year of the reign of Jehoiakim king of Judah"* (Daniel 1:1A). Who was Jehoiakim? Here is not a household name in our Bible knowledge. As we study the kings in Judah, we come to one by the name of Manasseh in 2 Chronicles 33. Manasseh reigned for fifty-five years in Jerusalem and turned his back on God. *"But he did that which was evil in the sight of the LORD, like unto the abominations of the heathen, whom the LORD had cast out before the children of Israel"* (2 Chronicles 33:2). Under his reign, the land slipped into heathen idolatrous worship and paid a huge price. God spoke to Manasseh and to the people, but they would not listen and so were attacked by the king of Assyria and carried into Babylon.

As a result of this chastening, Manasseh "humbled himself greatly before the God of his fathers." God heard his prayer and delivered the nation, but the damage was done in the hearts of the people. They never did return completely to the Lord. When Manasseh died, he was succeeded by his son Amon who only reigned two years but took the nation farther from God. It says in 2 Chronicles 33:23 that he *"…humbled not himself before the LORD as Manasseh his father had humbled himself; but Amon trespassed more and more."* Thus, his own servants conspired against him and slew him.

The nation was in a mess. Leadership had failed. God was being ignored, and compromise, conflict, and chaos followed. Second Chronicles 34 opens with Amon's son being thrust into leadership. Because of his father's untimely death, he was but eight years old! That in itself is startling, for how would an eight-year-old lead a nation in a calm moment, much less a chaotic time? But chapter 34 is a marvelous story of one of the greatest revivals on the pages of history. Josiah begins to seek after God while he is young and soon purges the land of the idols and false images. He annihilated not only the abominations throughout the land but the leaders who led in this pagan worship.

In this process of purging the land, he noticed that God's house was in shambles and needed repair and so he designated some money to repair the house of the Lord. In the process of restoring God's house, one day they discovered a book. A priest by the name of Hilkiah found this book and recognized it as "the book of the law given by Moses." Hilkiah delivered the book to Shaphan the scribe who took it to Josiah and read it before the king. Verse 19 records, *"And it came to pass, when the king had heard the words of the law, that he rent his clothes."* Truth had been attacked and tragedy resulted. In verse 21, Josiah commands: *"Go, enquire of the LORD for me, and for them that are left in Israel and in Judah, concerning the words of the book that is found: for great is the wrath of the LORD that is poured out upon us, because our fathers have not kept the word of the LORD, to do after all that is written in this book."*

King Josiah now called the nation back to the Truth and revival resulted in Judah. Josiah reigned for thirty-one years, and his legacy of returning the nation to Truth is stated clearly in the last verse of 2 Chronicles 34: *"And Josiah took away all the abominations out of all the countries that pertained to the children of Israel, and made all that were present in Israel to serve, even to serve the LORD their God. And all his days they departed not from following the LORD, the God of their fathers."*

With that stage now set, we go back to Daniel 1 and this man Jehoiakim. Jehoiakim was Josiah's son, and through some unusual events in the opening verses of 2 Chronicles 36, he becomes king over Judah. But he did not follow the steps of his father Josiah. *"Jehoiakim was twenty and five years old when he began to reign, and he reigned eleven years in Jerusalem: and he did that which was evil in the sight of the LORD his God"*

JUST BECAUSE WE DECIDE THAT WE ARE THROUGH WITH GOD DOES NOT MEAN THAT HE IS THROUGH WITH US.

(2 Chronicles 36:5). Just because one generation walks with God does not guarantee that the next one will. We don't inherit salvation (God has no grandchildren; only children) or godliness. *"There is a generation that curseth their father, and doth not bless their mother"* (Proverbs 30:11).

Jehoiakim knew better than to compromise. These kings studied their ancestors and their nation's history. He had heard and read about his great-grandfather Manasseh and his compromise. He knew about his grandfather Amon's rejection of God and he grew up in a time of great revival in the leader of that revival's house! But one thing we never learn from history is to learn from history. Truth can't be altered and Proverbs 14:34 makes it plain: *"Righteousness exalteth a nation: but sin is a reproach to any people."* And so Jehoiakim leads the nation in **A Departure**.

Compromise has a cost. This departure is followed by **A Devastation**. *"In the third year of the reign of Jehoiakim king of Judah came Nebuchadnezzar king of Babylon unto Jerusalem, and besieged it"* (Daniel 1:1). We may think we are exempt or above the devastation that comes with compromise, but Satan is no respecter of persons when he fires his darts. Of Jehoiakim it says in 2 Chronicles 36:6, *"Against him came up Nebuchadnezzar king of Babylon, and bound him in fetters, to carry him to Babylon."* Nebuchadnezzar may have been the most powerful ruler of all time. Daniel in chapter 5 is speaking to Belshazzar, the grandson of Nebuchadnezzar, and he says this about him: *"O thou king, the most high God gave Nebuchadnezzar thy father a kingdom, and a majesty, and glory, and honour: And for the majesty that he gave him, all people, nations, and languages, trembled and feared before him: whom he would he slew; and whom he would he kept alive; and whom he would he set up; and whom he would he put down"* (Daniel 5:18–19). All feared the name and authority of this powerful king. When we compromise Truth and depart, we become vulnerable to terrible and costly devastation.

God didn't create mindless robots but rather people who could think, reason, and choose. He gives us control over our own choices, but we are not in control of the consequences of those choices. *"If ye be willing and obedient, ye shall eat the good of the land: But if ye refuse and rebel, ye shall be devoured with the sword: for the mouth of the* LORD *hath spoken it"* (Isaiah 1:19–20). God's Word is Truth and *"Whoso despiseth the word shall be destroyed: but he that feareth the commandment shall be rewarded"* (Proverbs 13:13).

Often people will ask: "When will God judge America for her sins?" We think now of the decades of abortion, immorality, perverted lifestyles, and lawlessness and wonder, "Why isn't God doing something about all of this corruption?" We need to understand that the immorality, lawlessness, homosexuality, etc., *is* the punishment. Romans 1:21 reveals the "departure" from God: *"Because that, when they knew God, they glorified him not as God."* We know God in America. His name is on our currency and in our pledge of allegiance. Even with the re-writes of American history in recent days, it is hard to eliminate God from the records containing the founding of the United States. He is there over and over again with His divine providence, protection, and provision.

But when secular humanism infiltrated, America decided to ignore God. The Ten Commandments came down from the walls of our schools. Prayer was eliminated from public meetings. We decided we didn't need to live by God's Word because we had become enlightened to a better way of thinking and living. And when that takes place in a nation or a people, or even a church, the devastation is sure to follow as part of the judgment of God. What happened to those in Romans 1 who no longer acknowledged God and departed from Truth? *"For this cause God gave them up unto vile affections: for even their women did change the natural use into that which is against nature: And likewise also the men, leaving the natural use of the woman, burned in their lust one toward another; men with men working that which is unseemly, and receiving in themselves that recompence of their error which was meet. And even as they did not like to retain God in their knowledge, God gave them over to a reprobate mind, to do those things which are not convenient; Being filled with all unrighteousness, fornication, wickedness, covetousness, maliciousness; full of envy, murder, debate, deceit, malignity; whisperers, Backbiters, haters of God, despiteful, proud, boasters, inventors of evil things, disobedient to parents, Without understanding, covenantbreakers, without natural affection, implacable, unmerciful: Who knowing the judgment of God, that they which commit such things are worthy of death, not only do the same, but have pleasure in them that do them"* (Romans 1:26–32).

With that **Departure** and **Devastation**, comes then **A Desecration**. *"And the Lord gave Jehoiakim king of Judah into his hand, with part of the vessels of the house of God: which he carried into the land of Shinar to the house of his god; and he brought the vessels into the treasure house of his god"* (Daniel 1:2). These were vessels that had been carefully crafted and sacredly used in the house of God. Now they were taken down to Babylon and used to worship pagan gods. *"Nebuchadnezzar also carried of the vessels of the house of the LORD to Babylon, and put them in his temple at Babylon"* (2 Chronicles 36:7). God doesn't share His glory with anyone or anything. *"I am the LORD: that is my name: and my glory will I not give to another, neither my praise to graven images"* (Isaiah 42:8).

God has carefully planned and constructed three "vessels." These vessels, as I am choosing to call them here, have a distinct purpose given to them by their Creator. They were designed to carry out His purpose, and to desecrate them is a serious offense. God first designed the "vessel" or institution of the family. The home is God's first and foremost institution and was designed to be the primary place of instruction from God's Word (see Deuteronomy 6). Today, we can't even come to an agreement about the definition of marriage. The government was then instituted for the purpose of protecting those who obey God and punish the evil doers (see 1 Peter 2:14). Today the criminal is often protected by law and the God-fearing Christian punished. The local church is God's third vessel to carry out his work, and yet again today laws are being passed to silence her message and prosecute her ministers for hate crimes when in reality they are simply proclaiming the truth of God's Word.

As the book of Daniel opens, we are at the **End of Revival**. But don't lose hope. Just because we decide we are through with God does not mean that He is through with us.

AN EMERGING REMNANT

I found myself preaching one Sunday in Lander, Wyoming. After the morning services and lunch, the pastor asked me if I would like to get some exercise. He knew I enjoyed the outdoors and informed me that there was a beautiful canyon in their area and we could hike all afternoon if we wished. I gladly took him up on it and after changing clothes, began a rigorous but enjoyable journey.

The pastor was a Vietnam veteran, and he was on a mission to take me as far as we could in one afternoon. He established a fast pace and I did everything I could to keep up along a narrow trail. I noticed immediately that we were following a river that was flowing in the same direction that we were headed. After a couple of miles however, I noticed that the river had disappeared. After about a half mile or so, I asked the pastor what had happened to the river. We were in a canyon; it could not have exited or simply dried up. Looking over his shoulder, he said, "Oh, we'll see it again." I kept my mouth shut and kept hiking. After another mile or so, I again noticed the river flowing along side of us as it had when we first started. "Pastor," I said, "Now tell me something. First there was a river and then there wasn't. Now the river is back. I'm confused." He stopped and looked at me and confidently stated: "It was there the whole time. The river runs underground for about a mile. It was there, you just couldn't see it."

I pondered that natural phenomenon the rest of the hike and learned a powerful truth about God that day. God is always present, but there are times when we cannot see His work. I have learned since that God is often doing some of His greatest work during times when to us He seems to be silent. As the book of Daniel opens, revival has ended and God appears to be silently allowing departure, devastation, and desecration. Today, true revival seems a distant memory that is only read and studied in history books. Compromise is rampant and the world is seemingly on a one-way commute to destruction.

Take time to meditate on Ezra 9:8: *"And now for a little space grace hath been shewed from the LORD our God, to leave us a remnant to escape, and to give us a nail in his holy place, that our God may lighten our eyes, and give us a little reviving in our bondage.*" Space for grace! That's why God always leaves a remnant no matter how dark the hour. He leaves a space for the remnant to be used to lead once again in great revival.

In Daniel 1:3, we see the river that had been flowing underground for a time reappearing as **The Purpose of God** is revealed. *"And the king spake unto Ashpenaz the master of his eunuchs, that he should bring certain of the children of Israel, and of the king's seed, and of the princes."* Nothing ever just happens with God. There are no accidents but rather a careful orchestrated purpose and plan. And we can always be sure that His plan will be perfect. *"As for God, his way is perfect: the word of the LORD is tried: he is a buckler to all those that trust in him"* (Psalm 18:30). God makes no mistakes as He accomplishes His purpose in us. *"The LORD is righteous in all his ways, and holy in all his works"* (Psalm 145:17).

We are only able to see life from the playing field, but God sees it from the blimp. Our human inability does not allow us to see as He sees and knows. No matter what is happening in our lives, He will always see us through to the purpose that He has established. *"For I know the thoughts that I think toward you, saith the LORD, thoughts of peace, and not of evil, to give you an expected end"* (Jeremiah 29:11). If we will stay focused on loving Him and serving Him, God will lead us through the maze of life in an amazing and exciting way. *"And we know that all things work together for good to them that love God, to them who are the called according to his purpose"* (Romans 8:28). You can trust God's purpose for your life.

Within the purpose of God we begin to see **The Preparation of the Godly** unfolding. *"Children in whom was no blemish, but* *well favoured, and skilful in all wisdom, and cunning in knowledge, and understanding science, and such as had ability in them to stand in the king's palace, and whom they might teach the learning and the tongue of the Chaldeans*" (Daniel 1:4). God's people were uprooted from their homeland and carried away as captives into Babylon, but within this company, God had a group of young men that He was preparing for a great work. When God has a work to do, He looks for people with ability—availability, pliability, and dependability. God can prepare your life in an awesome way if you are willing.

King Nebuchadnezzar was looking for some of these captives who could be trained in the way of the heathen, but God had already prepared them. They were men who were exercised in body, educated in mind, and excellent in spirit. Are you allowing God to prepare your life for "such a time as this?" Esther was another Bible character who lived during a time of great testing. Things were changing all around her and the people of God were in danger of extinction. But God prepared Esther and then put her in the exact place where she could be used to deliver the nation.

God saved you for such a time as this. He has placed you in your city, at your job, and in your local church for such a time as this. He has given you influence to use for Him in such a time as this. Esther thought that she was insignificant. Joseph didn't understand his mistreatment. Daniel no doubt wondered why his country was ransacked and he was carried off as a slave, but God was preparing each of these for His purpose.

The unsaved world has no regard for God and His purpose. Satan and his forces try to influence and intimidate God's people.

He makes us think that God is unreliable in tough times and that our dependence is on him for survival. Thus, in Daniel 1:5–7, we see **The Provision of Godlessness.** *"And the king appointed them a daily provision of the king's meat, and of the wine which he drank: so nourishing them three years, that at the end thereof they might stand before the king. Now among these were of the children of Judah, Daniel, Hananiah, Mishael, and Azariah: Unto whom the prince of the eunuch gave names: for he gave unto Daniel the name of Belteshazzar; and to Hananiah, of Sahdrach; and to Mishael, of Meshach; and to Azariah, of Abednego."*

The Babylonian leadership changed Daniel's name but they could not change his nature. Sadly, many Christians look to the world to meet their needs rather than to God. Even more sad is the fact that many churches today feel the need to resort to worldly means to build God's church. Schools seek the world's approval but concern themselves little with whether God is glorified and pleased. When credibility with culture is the goal, compromise is sure to follow. God

BABYLON CHANGED DANIEL'S NAME BUT THEY COULDN'T CHANGE HIS NATURE.

makes it clear as to where our trust must be in Psalm 118:8–9: *"It is better to trust in the Lord than to put confidence in man. It is better to trust in the Lord than to put confidence in princes."* In fact, we are on dangerous ground when we seek approval from man rather than God. *"Thus saith the Lord; Cursed be the man that trusteth in man, and maketh flesh his arm, and whose heart departeth from the Lord"* (Jeremiah 17:5).

When trouble comes and times are changing and we are tempted to compromise, we must look to the Lord as never before. *"God is our refuge and strength, a very present help in trouble. Therefore will not we fear, though the earth be removed, and though the mountains be carried into the midst of the sea; Though the waters*

GOOD HABITS ARE
PRODUCED FROM
GROUNDED HEARTS.

thereof roar and be troubled, though the mountains shake with the swelling thereof. Selah. There is a river, the streams whereof shall make glad the city of God, the holy place of the tabernacles of the most High. God is in the midst of her; she shall not be moved: God shall help her, and that right early" (Psalm 46:1–5). The psalmist knew where to look in time of need. It wasn't to the world system or to government. Our eyes must rise above the powers of earth. *"I will lift up mine eyes unto the hills, from whence cometh my help. My help cometh from the LORD, which made heaven and earth. He will not suffer thy foot to be moved; he that keepeth thee will not slumber. Behold, he that keepeth Israel shall neither slumber nor sleep. The LORD is thy keeper: the LORD is thy shade upon thy right hand. The sun shall not smite thee by day, nor the moon by night. The LORD shall preserve thee from all evil: he shall preserve thy soul. The LORD shall preserve thy going out and thy coming in from this time forth, and even for evermore"* (Psalm 121:1–8).

God is always working. While one generation may be at **An End of Revival**, God is preparing **An Emerging Remnant**.

AN EMPHATIC RESISTANCE

The hour is bleak as God's people have been carried into Babylon and are now slaves in the palace of the most powerful king of all time. Their leaders were destroyed; they are surrounded by paganism; as captives they have no rights or privileges; and they are being forced into a position of compromise. *"But Daniel…"* (Daniel 1:8A). Don't you love that? But Daniel! He was not in the majority and the momentum was not on the side of God's people, but Daniel had **A Purposed Heart**. *"But Daniel purposed in his heart that he would not defile himself with the portion of the king's meat, nor with the wine which he drank"* (Daniel 1:8A).

Good habits are produced from grounded hearts. The tests will come, and your testimony in those tests will be determined by the template of right and wrong in your heart. We often wonder why we are so weak in times of testing. We are doing so good in the class of Christianity until exam day and then we compromise. The exams of life can only be passed as we allow entrance of God's Word into our hearts. *"Thy word have I hid in mine heart, that I might not sin against thee"* (Psalm 119:11). Solomon knew that his son would face tests in life and so wisely gave him instruction on how to study for the final exam. *"My son, keep thy father's commandment, and forsake not the law of thy mother: Bind them continually upon thine heart, and tie them about thy neck. When thou goest, it shall lead thee; when thou sleepest, it shall keep thee; and when thou awakest, it shall talk with thee. For the commandment is a lamp; and the law is a light; and the reproofs of instruction are the way of life"* (Proverbs 6:20–23).

Every generation faces tests and has the opportunity to compromise. As leaders today, we must set the pace for those coming after us. Children follow their parents; people follow their pastors; new Christians follow the older; and so on. As twenty-first century Christians, we are facing some tests and how we respond will influence the next generation. *"By faith Moses, when he was born, was hid three months of his parents, because they saw he was a proper child; and they were not afraid of the king's commandment. By faith Moses, when he was come to years, refused to be called the son of Pharaoh's daughter; Choosing rather to suffer the affliction with the people of God, than to enjoy the pleasures of sin for a season; Esteeming the reproach of Christ greater riches than the treasures in Egypt: for he had respect unto the recompense of the reward. By faith he forsook Egypt, not fearing the wrath of the king: for he endured, as seeing him who is invisible"* (Hebrew 11:23–27). Neither compromise nor obedience only affects you.

Daniel backs up **A Purposed Heart** with **A Pure Hand.** *"Now God had brought Daniel into favour and tender love with the prince of the eunuchs"* (Daniel 1:9). No one respects the purpose of our heart if it is not backed up by a pure hand. The world doesn't respect talk without walk. Our theology must be mixed with life. Good beliefs without good behavior never impacts the world. Peter admonishes us in 1 Peter 2:11–12 to have a pure hand: *"Dearly beloved, I beseech you as strangers and pilgrims, abstain from fleshly lusts, which war against the soul; Having your conversation honest among the Gentiles: that, whereas they speak evil against you as evildoers, they may by your good works, which they shall behold, glorify God in the day of visitation."* Peter was merely re-preaching the message he had heard on the Mount of Olives: *"Ye are the light*

ALL OF THE WHAT'S, THE WHERE'S, AND THE HOW'S OF LIFE ARE A RISK UNTIL YOU KNOW THE WHO.

of the world. A city that is set on an hill cannot be hid. Neither do men light a candle, and put it under a bushel, but on a candlestick; and it giveth light unto all that are in the house. Let your light so shine before men, that they may see your good works, and glorify your Father which is in heaven" (Matthew 5:14–16).

During my first year in evangelism, I didn't have meetings every week, and so I worked at Manpower, Inc. (a temporary work service) every time I was home to keep food on the table. They would often send me to a place called Vitamins, Inc. in Michigan City, Indiana. They would hire guys to unload and load railroad cars all day. Train cars filled with one hundred pound bags of wheat germ would arrive daily and had to be unloaded by hand. The wheat germ was put through some kind of process in that plant and then re-bagged and shipped to Battle Creek, Michigan where it was made into various types of cereal.

I worked with a rough crowd, but being raised on a farm and playing football through college, I enjoyed the work because it helped keep me in shape. It was a union plant and so they always took a morning break at ten o'clock and an afternoon break at three. On the first day that I worked there I went into the break room with the guys but immediately was subjected to a host of dirty stories and jokes. I determined after that first ten-minute break that I would never return to the break room. At three that afternoon, I just sat down out in the railroad car and rested. Of course the questions came as to why. I told them that I was a Christian and didn't want my mind to be filled with ungodly thoughts. I didn't preach to them or condemn them; I just quietly took my stand.

I expected the ridicule and the teasing, but I did not expect the scrutiny. From that point on, they were constantly trying to catch me doing something that would compromise my testimony. I knew that I had to be extremely careful. One of the older men that worked there was quiet toward me, but I could tell he hated my Christianity. He would often make demands of me and curse me just to see what my reaction would be. I really didn't have to face him too often as he worked in a lab building across the property all by himself.

One day I was instructed by my boss Mr. Gill to get a dolly and take a barrel of wheat oil over to that lab where this man worked. I secured the dolly and loaded the barrel and began to wheel it across the parking lot. As I entered the door into that lab to deliver that barrel, I was shocked! Plastered on the walls over every square inch of that lab were pornographic pictures. As soon as my eyes made contact with this filth, I looked down focusing on the dolly and the barrel in front of me. I could "feel" that man's eyes from across the room as he watched me the entire time. As best I could, I kept my eyes off of those pictures for the five minutes or so that I was in that lab. Guess what? From that time on, that man never made fun of me again. He even defended me when the other guys called me "preacher" or some less complimentary term. Believe me, there have been other times where I wasn't as vigilant in my walk, but by the grace of God on that occasion, my walk had backed up my talk. Daniel had **A Purposed Heart** backed up by **A Pure Hand**.

AN EARNEST REQUEST

Daniel has been taken into captivity. In all likelihood his parents have been killed in the raid. He is now placed in a pagan culture and commanded to participate in things that were forbidden. He is being forced to compromise his life. But there is no bitterness or anger displayed in his disposition as he takes his position. Rather, we see **A Cordial Resolve**. When the tide turns against you it is easy to get upset, frustrated, and angry. But as Peter reminds us, this is our opportunity to identify with our Saviour. *"For this is thankworthy, if a man for conscience toward God endure grief, suffering wrongfully. For what glory is it, if, when ye be buffeted for your faults, ye shall take it patiently? but if when ye do well, and suffer for it, ye take it patiently, this is acceptable with God. For even hereunto were ye called: because Christ also suffered for us, leaving us an example, that ye should follow in his steps"* (1 Peter 2:19–21).

One of the great statements about Jesus Christ is found in John 1:14, where the Bible says, *"And the Word was made flesh, and dwelt among us, (and we beheld his glory, the glory as of the only begotten of the Father,) full of grace and truth."* What balance—Full of grace and truth! Often, when I have a lot of grace there isn't much truth and when I know I'm right, I don't have a whole lot of grace. We need to have the right spirit in these days as we uncompromisingly take our position. It was said of C.H. Spurgeon that "his greatness was in his inherent goodness." Unquestionably, this was the message that Paul was conveying to the church at Ephesus when he reminds us to be *"…speaking the truth in love"* (Ephesians 4:15).

Coupled with this **Cordial Resolve** was **A Clean Resumé**. Daniel 1:9 tells us that Daniel was brought into favour with the prince of the eunuchs. Backing up his resolve to do right was a resumé that was without hypocrisy. Later on in the book of Daniel, we see where his enemies tried to find some flaw on his record. *"Then this Daniel was preferred above the presidents and princes, because an excellent spirit was in him; and the king thought to set him over the whole realm. Then the presidents and princes sought to find occasion against Daniel concerning the kingdom; but they could find none occasion nor fault; forasmuch as he was faithful, neither was there any error or fault found in him"* (Daniel 6:3–4). What an outstanding resumé for God.

Our testimony needs to give people the right opinion about God. It may not always seem fair but, *"Ye are our epistle written in our hearts, known and read of all men: Forasmuch as ye are manifestly declared to be the epistle of Christ ministered by us, written not with ink, but with the Spirit of the living God; not in tables of stone, but in fleshy tables of the heart"* (2 Corinthians 3:2–3). In Philippians 1:27, Paul adds, *"Only let your conversation be as it becometh the gospel of Christ: that whether I come and see you, or else be absent, I may hear of your affairs, that ye stand fast in one spirit, with one mind striving together for the faith of the gospel."* The word "Christian" means "Christ-like." If the only thing someone knew about Christianity is what they saw in your life, what would their opinion be of God? Most people never read the Bible and many never hear a sermon, but they do watch our lives. What message have we given them?

In verse 10 we see **A Concerned Reluctance**. *"And the prince of the eunuchs said unto Daniel, I fear my lord the king, who hath* *appointed your meat and your drink: for why should he see your faces worse liking than the children which are of your sort? then shall ye make me endanger my head to the king."* We should never be surprised by the world's skepticism. For the child of God, faith should come easy. After all, if God can forgive all of our sins and give us eternal life in heaven rather than hell, why couldn't that God give us health and strength from vegetables rather

GOD IS LOOKING FOR CHAMPIONS NOT CHAMELEONS.

than meat? To Daniel, his request was not far-fetched, but to the prince of the eunuchs it was absurd, not to mention dangerous! This man knew the fate of those who disobeyed Nebuchadnezzar, and while he respected Daniel highly, it wasn't worth his life to disobey.

God is not shocked that lost people act lost (He is shocked when saved people act lost.). This prince could not comprehend risking your life for religious convictions. *"But the natural man receiveth not the things of the Spirit of God: for they are foolishness unto him: neither can he know them, because they are spiritually discerned"* (1 Corinthians 2:14). Your unbending convictions will not make sense to a lost culture when compromise would be so much more comfortable. God however, did not call us to be comfortable; He called us to conform to His image.

Daniel is willing to take **A Confident Risk**. *"Then said Daniel to Melzar, whom the prince of the eunuchs had set over Daniel, Hananiah, Mishael, and Azariah, Prove thy servants, I beseech thee, ten days; and let them give us pulse to eat, and water to drink. Then let our countenances be looked upon before thee, and the countenance of the children that eat of the portion of the king's* *meat: and as thou seest, deal with thy servants. So he consented to them in this matter, and proved them ten days"* (Daniel 1:11–14). Now I know that the words confident and risk do not seem to fit together. All of the what's, the where's, and the how's of life are a risk until you know the Who. It made absolutely no sense humanly to believe that vegetables and water would make one stronger than eating the finest of protein and drinking the best of wine in the king's palace. It wasn't the diet but the Divine that made the difference!

God is absolutely sick of our blame shifting, rationalization, and excuses for compromise. We have focused our eyes on our environment instead of the eternal. We are more concerned about what culture thinks than we are of what Christ thinks. We are willing to trust the government but not God. People blame their sin on their background, past experiences, or current relationships. Churches blame their compromise on the lack of results, governmental pressure, or the hedonistic culture. God is bigger than broken homes, economic collapse, tyrannous governments, and moral decay.

After preaching on revival one night, a friend of mine came to me and said, "John, every time I hear you preach on revival it sounds as though you actually believe we can have another great national working of God. What do you see that gives you hope that such a revival could take place?" I thought a moment, and said: "Nothing. I don't see anything that gives me hope that we could have revival. In fact, I see just the opposite. But I don't have to see it to believe that it could happen." The Bible admonishes us to *"…walk by faith, not by sight"* (2 Corinthians 5:7B).

Faith is all about taking some confident risks. Nothing in Hebrews 11 made sense humanly. It didn't make sense to build an ark when it had never rained; march around a city without weapons and expect the walls to fall; or attempt to kill a giant with a slingshot. But each verse of that Hall of Faith begins with "by faith." In this age of technology we want to see everything. We want to preview before we print. We want God to put His plan up on a screen so that we can study it, scrutinize it, and alter it! We want to delete what we can't figure out or what doesn't make sense. At the very least we want to cut and paste what we can't understand to a later time.

God says: *"But without faith it is impossible to please him: for he that cometh to God must believe that he is, and that he is a rewarder of them that diligently seek him"* (Hebrews 11:6). It doesn't say it is improbable to please Him, or unlikely, but impossible! The Apostle Paul was very blunt about this matter of sight-walking versus faith living. *"And he that doubteth is damned if he eat, because he eateth not of faith: for whatsoever is not of faith is sin"* (Romans 14:23). To live by what we can see, plan, contrive, or figure out is to live in sin. We have way too many "boat-riders" and not enough "water-walkers." If you can't trust God, you will soon be relying on yourself. That is a sure recipe for compromise.

AN EFFECTUAL RESILIENCE

Through this era of tumultuous change, God brings forth a triumphant champion. No one prays for chaotic and confusing times. We would much rather serve the Lord with as few obstacles as possible. But God doesn't sharpen iron with wood. God uses the difficult times to shape and fashion His servants. *"Behold, I have refined thee, but not with silver; I have chosen thee in the furnace of affliction"* (Isaiah 48:10). Think about that the next time you are in a battle. God goes to the furnace of affliction to find those that He will use. Job understood this timeless principle. *"But he knoweth the way that I take: when he hath tried me, I shall come forth as gold"* (Jobs 23:10).

In the midst of this difficult time, Daniel exhibits **A Pleasing Faith**. God always honors and blesses faith. *"And at the end of ten days their countenances appeared fairer and fatter in flesh than all the children which did eat the portion of the king's meat"* (Daniel 1:15). You can compromise when the pressure comes, but God will honor you if you will by faith trust Him and obey His Word. How big is your God? Can He not meet your needs? Can He not build His church? *"But seek ye first the kingdom of God, and his righteousness; and all these things shall be added unto you"* (Matthew 6:33). The psalmist David speaks from his own experience in Psalm 37:23–25: *"The steps of a good man are ordered by the LORD: and he delighteth in his way. Though he fall, he shall not be utterly cast down: for the LORD upholdeth him with his hand. I have been young, and now am old; yet have I not seen the righteous forsaken, nor his seed begging bread."*

This pleasing faith of Daniel led to **A Promoted Favor**. I love the results of this story in Daniel 1. Daniel refuses to compromise his convictions and trusts God by faith to take care of him. But God doesn't just preserve Daniel, He promotes him! *"Thus Melzar took away the portion of their meat, and the* *wine that they should drink; and gave them pulse. As for these four children, God gave them knowledge and skill in all learning and wisdom: and Daniel had understanding in all visions and dreams. Now at the end of the days that the king had said he should bring them in, then the prince of the eunuchs brought them in before Nebuchadnezzar. And the king communed with them; and among them all was found none like Daniel, Hananiah, Mishael, and Azariah: therefore stood they before the king. And in all matters of wisdom and understanding, that the king enquired of them, he found them ten times better than all the magicians and astrologers that were in all his realm"* (Daniel 1:16–20).

Three years have gone by, and all four of these Hebrew slaves have remained faithful to their God. No doubt the others in training questioned their commitment and wondered why they chose not to compromise their convictions. But God didn't just help them survive; He made them superlative! They didn't simply graduate at the top of their class—they totally ruined the curve! In every area of their preparation, they were ten times better than the rest. God indeed takes the foolish things to confound the wise.

This **Pleasing Faith** and **Promoted Favor** led Daniel to **A Preserved Finish**. Daniel 1 closes with these words in verse 21: *"And Daniel continued even unto the first year of King Cyrus."* Daniel outlived Nebuchadnezzar! Daniel could have been executed at the time of the besieging of Jerusalem with many of his friends and family members. Any time during this process, he could have lost his life for staying true to His God. But Daniel triumphed in the midst of turmoil. Why? How? Because *"Ye are of God, little children, and have overcome them: because greater* *is he that is in you, than he that is in the world"* (1 John 4:4). Philippians 1:6 reminds us that *"Being confident of this very thing, that he which hath begun a good work in you will perform it until the day of Jesus Christ."*

When the world calls for change and Satan tempts us with compromise, God is looking for champions! Not chameleons but champions. Changing times produce a lot of chameleons. The world is their standard, and as the world changes they blend their convictions with the culture. God is looking for champions who will meet the test as David against Goliath of old saying, *"The battle is the Lord's"* (1 Samuel 17:47).

The tests will come to every generation and so will the temptation to compromise our convictions. We can blend with the world or depend on God and His Word.

One night when I was nine years old, we finished up the milking and chores in the barn around seven o'clock. As we got to the house, instead of our usual family time and a bowl of cereal, my sister and I were sent to bed. It was still light outside and impossible to go to sleep. I remember laying in my bed wondering if we were being punished for something. Suddenly, I heard a car drive in the gravel driveway outside. I ran to the third-story window of that farmhouse and to my glee discovered that my grandparents had arrived. And behind them were two of my Uncles and Aunts. My sister had made the same discovery and so both of us ran to the top of the stairway and waited on the top step knowing that we would soon be called downstairs for this unexpected family gathering.

That call never came. Instead, when the door was opened and family members entered, there were no usual greetings and handshakes. As my sister and I peeked around the corner, we could see that everyone had gone quietly into the living room and were seated in a circle. I heard my grandfather say, "Marvin, [my dad] you need to stay in the church. We need you. You're a leader there. Please don't go." My uncles both joined in with this appeal. My sister and I looked at each other in bewilderment.

My dad sat in the midst of our closest relatives and said: "I'm sorry, I would like to stay, but we can't. The church is going in a wrong direction, and we must leave." The silence that followed was broken only by the sobbing of the ladies. Finally after about an hour, some terse good-byes were said, and everyone left. My sister and I never asked about that momentous meeting in our living room. My grandfather as a layman had joined with seven other men and started that First Baptist Church where we were members. That old Northern Baptist Church in its early history experienced the hand of God and a measure of revival. I have fond memories of Sunday school classes, Vacation Bible Schools, and church services in that old rickety building in Watertown, Wisconsin. I remember an old white-haired man by the name of Victor who used to let me climb up into the steeple and help him ring the bell for Sunday services. I recall the fiery preaching of evangelists, missionaries, and of course our pastor.

But the test came and my dad decided that he could no longer compromise with the liberalism and modernism that had crept into that congregation. The next Sunday we found ourselves in the basement of a house at a service being conducted by a church planter by the name of Grant Rice. On my tenth birthday, my dad and mom joined Calvary Baptist Church. I didn't know then the difference between the Northern Baptists, the Southern Baptists, or the Independent Baptists, but I'm glad my dad did. Many of our family members remained at First Baptist Church and my cousins went off to liberal schools and became ministers in new evangelical churches. By the time my grandmother passed away a few years later, I could not even discern the Bible version they were reading in the service. Sunday night services disappeared from their schedule and a social gospel was soon the mission.

From that point on, the family reunions and gatherings were never quite the same. To be honest, it was difficult and unpleasant to me at times. I didn't like the fact that we didn't all go to the same church any longer. But I'm glad now that my dad was a champion rather than a chameleon. He could have blended in with the change, and at age ten I would never have known the difference. But my course would have been vastly different. No test is easy, but the future generations depend on whether we pass or fail. The next generation is far too valuable for us to compromise.

CONCLUSION

As West Coast Baptist College has grown, we have discovered the need to collect, store, and use accurate data. In the early days when we had less than fifty students that information could easily be stored in my brain. I knew where each student was from, what their major was, what kind of car they drove, how much they owed on their school bill, and whether or not they liked Chinese food! Now we have met thousands of high school students interested in the college. Hundreds come for training or are in our online programs, and several hundred more have graduated and are serving around the world. Neither my brain nor that of our dozens of staff members has been able to keep up.

With that growth in numbers we have developed many different departments to assist in keeping track of all of the information. The recruiting office, the Dean's office, the advancement office, the finance office, the employment office, the registrar's office, the academic office, the alumni office, the records department, etc. all help in tracking each young person as they enroll, attend, and then graduate to serve the Lord. This multiplicity of offices, with each containing pieces of information, made it difficult to create a complete and accurate picture of each student. Sometimes the data would even be conflicting in nature.

This problem that developed from the growth of our school led us to finding a Student Management System that could keep, sort, and manage all of this information. Our team went to work and investigated several companies and two of them came and presented their product to us. We eventually selected one of these companies, and now we can send an email to all of the left-handed, red-haired, juniors, who are unmarried mission majors, if we so desire! It is an amazing system. The system takes any and all of the information and makes it accessible to us at any time.

When the representative of this system made his presentation to us, he used a term that immediately caught my attention. He said, "This system will provide your ministry with a 'single version of truth.'" In other words, instead of getting one piece of information from one data base used in the finance department and a different data base used in the Dean's office and having to piece them together in order to build a student profile, we would be able to go to one system, type in a name and instantly have accurate information about every area of that student's life. Having one source of truth eliminated all kinds of inaccurate data and simplified everything.

I'm sure glad that God has not given us multi-versions of truth concerning Himself or His direction for our lives. Ephesians 4:6 declares that there is *"One God and Father of all, who is above all, and through all, and in you all."* The devil, however, is working tirelessly to hack into that single version of Truth in order to compromise all God is and what He has said in His Word.

In Exodus 5 we find the Israelites in bondage in the land of Egypt. The land of Egypt in the Old Testament is a type of sin and the world. God does not want His people living in the world, and so He sent Moses and Aaron to Pharaoh. *"And afterward Moses and Aaron went in, and told Pharaoh, Thus saith the* LORD *God of Israel, Let my people go, that they may hold a feast unto me in the wilderness. And Pharaoh said, Who is the* LORD, *that I should obey his voice to let Israel go? I know not the* LORD, *neither will I let Israel go. And they said, The God of the Hebrews hath met with us: let us go, we pray thee, three days' journey into the desert, and sacrifice unto the* LORD *our God; lest he fall upon us with pestilence, or with the sword"* (Exodus 5:1–3).

Because Pharaoh would not listen, God sent plagues upon the land of Egypt to force them to release the Israelites. As these plagues began to fall, Pharaoh called for Moses and Aaron wanting to negotiate with them. In Exodus 8:25, it says: *"And Pharaoh called for Moses and for Aaron, and said, Go ye, sacrifice to your God in the land."* God wanted His people to separate from Egypt and worship Him out in the desert. Pharaoh tried to talk them into worshipping God right there in Egypt. He tempted them to compromise by offering them a **Cultural God**. Many people today want to mix God and the world together. We attach the name Christian to everything from rock music to homosexuality. God and this world's culture have absolutely nothing in common. *"For all that is in the world, the lust of the flesh, and the lust of the eyes, and the pride of life, is not of the Father, but is of the world"* (1 John 2:16).

A few verses later, when Moses would not compromise and worship a cultural God, Pharaoh offered him a **Convenient God**. *"And Pharaoh said, I will let you go, that ye may sacrifice to the LORD your God in the wilderness; only ye shall not go very far away"* (Exodus 8:28A). Go ahead and leave the world but don't go too far. That way, if things get tough you can always return. Many Christians today try to stay as close to the "line" of separation as they can. They don't want to appear too fanatical and while they may align with Truth for a while they soon drift back into Egypt.

By Exodus 10, the plagues are in full swing and Pharaoh demands to see Moses and Aaron again. After a brief discussion about who will be going, Pharaoh decides to let them leave but then changes his mind in the middle of a sentence and offers them a **Confined God**. *"And he said unto them, Let the LORD be so with you, as I will let you go, and your little ones: look to it; for evil is before you. Not so: go now ye that are men, and serve the LORD; for that ye did desire. And they were driven out from Pharaoh's presence"* (Exodus 10:10–11). He agrees initially but then changes his mind and puts some restrictions on their request. Today, many allow God into their lives in some areas, but not all. They want to dictate to God where He can be God and leave the rest of life to their own understanding.

At the end of chapter 10 we see Pharaoh offering a **Comfortable God**. *"And Pharaoh called unto Moses, and said, Go ye, serve the* LORD; *only let your flocks and your herds be stayed: let your little ones also go with you. And Moses said, Thou must give us also sacrifices and burnt offerings, that we may sacrifice unto the* LORD *our God. Our cattle also shall go with us; there shall not an hoof be left behind; for thereof must we take to serve the* LORD *our God; and we know not with what we must serve the* LORD, *until we come thither"* (Exodus 10:24–26). It would have been easier to leave the animals in Egypt, but they would have had nothing to offer the Lord in sacrifice. Today, we want a salvation without the cost of repentance of sin and Christianity without the cost of a commitment.

Moses and Aaron would not compromise their God and His Word. They kept repeating what they had stated in the beginning: *"We will go three days journey into the wilderness, and sacrifice to the* LORD *our God, as he shall command us"* (Exodus 8:27). The devil is the master at complimenting us about our God and His Word. But slowly and surely he will tell us that we really don't need everything about God and hold to every Truth in His Word. Little by little, we take the saw to our once beautiful sign: "Fresh Fish For Sale Today" and chop off a piece here and piece there until we don't need the sign at all.

Years ago the captain of a ship looked out over the vast ocean in front of him into the night sky. In the distance he noticed a light directly in the path of his massive boat. He commanded his signal man to send a message, "Alter your course ten degrees north." A few moments passed and a message was received in return, "Alter your course ten degrees south." The captain was not happy that his message was being ignored. He sent a second message, "Alter your course ten degrees north; I am a Captain!" After a few moments a second message was received, "Alter your course ten degrees south; I am seaman third class Jones." The captain was infuriated. He could not believe this response. He sent a third message knowing the fear that it would evoke, "Alter your course ten degrees north; I am a battleship!" After a pause, a third message was received, "Alter your course ten degrees south: I am a lighthouse."

You can spend the rest of your life trying to get God to move, but He is changeless. He's not moving! He is God. His Truth stands and will forever. We must not compromise the Truth of God. Others have lived and died for that Truth. Because they did, we have received that Truth. May we take the baton that has been passed to us, live faithfully the Truth we have been given, and by all means pass it on faithfully to those who are coming after us in the race that God has given us to run.

APPENDIX I

TWO CHURCHES
IN CONTRAST

EXCERPT FROM **THE SAVIOUR SENSITIVE CHURCH**
BY DR. PAUL CHAPPELL AND DR. JOHN GOETSCH

BIBLICAL MINISTRY VS.
MAN-CENTERED MINISTRY

In 1986, my wife and I left a wonderful church in northern California and drove a Ryder moving van to northern Los Angeles County to begin working with a small group of people to re-establish the Lancaster Baptist Church. I vividly recall the first Saturday night in Lancaster, as Terrie and I sat in the living room of our two-bedroom apartment, and constructed the first church bulletin. There was not much to say about the activities of the church because there were very few to announce! I decided it would be an opportune time to list some of the distinctives of the church in the bulletin.

In the bulletin we stated that Lancaster Baptist Church was an independent, fundamental, Bible-believing, separated Baptist church. With a strong doctrinal position and a heart for souls, we began preaching the Word of God fervently, and sharing the Gospel passionately in our community.

After being at the church a few Sundays, I distinctively remember after a service a man saying to me, "You cannot build a church in Southern California this way. This type of preaching and the old-fashioned music will no longer work. Churches that are growing in California will only grow if they use rock 'n roll music and a less emphatic preaching style."

As a young, zealous (and probably somewhat insecure) pastor, I remember telling the man distinctly that the word "preach" in the New Testament involved a strong declaration of the truth and that the singing of the church has always included psalms, hymns and "spiritual" songs. I told him that there were several churches down the street from us who would probably be glad to accommodate his desire, but that we intended to hold to our position.

It is interesting to study the early New Testament churches. In the letters to the churches, I find that each one apparently had a different personality, as well as a different spiritual fervor. Some churches were noble to search the Scriptures. Others seemed to disregard the early admonitions of the apostles.

Few churches in the New Testament can be contrasted like the church of Laodicea and the church of Thessalonica. In Revelation 2 and 3, we see the Lord speaking to the seven literal churches of Asia Minor. Each of these churches also seems to be a type of the seven stages of church history. The last church, the church of Laodicea, is of interesting note for the discerning Christian.

A short study of the etymology of the word "laodicea" shows the meaning to be "the people's rights." The Laodicean church was the church of the people's rights. Revelation 3:14 indicates the church was referred to as, *"the church of the Laodiceans"* rather than "the church of Laodicea." It was, indeed, the people's church. The people's rights were pre-eminent. In many ways this was the first seeker-sensitive church in church history.

No God-fearing pastor would desire his church to reflect the characteristics of the Laodicean church. Yet slowly, and sometimes like a frog in the kettle, unknowingly, good churches are being affected by the poor and unbiblical philosophies being taught at many seminars today.

Even George Barna, a Christian pollster, recently said in an interview, "I am really concerned about complacency among our churches. We are the church of Laodicea. We think we are hot stuff. We think the world takes its cues from us. We think we are tight with God, but really we don't have a clue."[1]

The church at Thessalonica stands in stark contrast to the church of Laodicea. Thessalonica was located about one hundred miles from Philippi on the Egnation Highway. Though the Apostle Paul had initially only been there for a few weeks, the Holy Spirit moved mightily, as he proclaimed the Gospel in this strategic location.

In 1 Thessalonians 1:3, Paul later wrote to the church and said, *"Remembering without ceasing your work of faith, and*

---

1.   *SBC Life Magazine,* June 2004 edition

labour of love, and patience of hope in our Lord Jesus Christ, in
the sight of God and our Father;"

Notice with me, some of the early characteristics of this
church and of Paul's ministry at Thessalonica. In 1 Thessalonians 1
and 2, the Apostle Paul is defending the integrity of his ministry
at Thessalonica and defining the qualities of the Saviour-
sensitive church.

A CHURCH WITH PURE MOTIVES

First of all, we learn that the church at Thessalonica was a church
with pure motives.

> *For our exhortation was not of deceit, nor of uncleanness,*
> *nor in guile: But as we were allowed of God to be put in*
> *trust with the gospel, even so we speak; not as pleasing*
> *men, but God, which trieth our hearts. For neither at*
> *any time used we flattering words, as ye know, nor a*
> *cloke of covetousness; God is witness: Nor of men sought*
> *we glory, neither of you, nor yet of others, when we*
> *might have been burdensome, as the apostles of Christ.*
> —1 THESSALONIANS 2:3–6

We sense that, as Paul defends the integrity of the church
at Thessalonica, he is aware that if his enemies could awaken
distrust concerning him as a messenger, it would bring distrust
to the message. Therefore, he very carefully shows us the motives
of his ministry in that city.

He first reminded the Thessalonicans that his ministry had
not been a deceitful one, or a ministry "in guile." The temples at
Thessalonica were definitely places of deceit. People attended a

temple, perhaps desiring to draw closer to God, but in fact, the end result was the opposite.

In the same way, much of the philosophy of the seeker-sensitive movement is deceitful. Churches are telling people to come just as they are, and stay as they are! They play the world's music, tell the world's jokes, encourage people to continue the way they want to live, and generally, tell people that there is no need for outward change in the Christian life.

The deceitfulness of this is found in the scriptural admonition from Romans 12:2, which says, *"And be not conformed to this world: but be ye transformed by the renewing of your mind, that ye may prove what is that good, and acceptable, and perfect, will of God."* Furthermore, in 2 Corinthians 5:17, the apostle says, *"Therefore if any man be in Christ, he is a new creature: old things are passed away; behold, all things are become new."*

To attract a crowd to church by encouraging them to come just as they are and leave without any change is to practice a kind of Christianity foreign to the teaching of the Bible.

Second, the Apostle Paul stated that he was not unclean in his ministry. Paul was a morally pure man. Paul stated that his ministry was not in guile. The word *guile* means "to bait or to snare." It speaks of using trickery or deceit.

When the term "new evangelicalism" was coined at Fuller Seminary by Harold Ockenga, his desire was to bring the modernists (deniers of the truth) together with the fundamentalists (believers of the truth) by encouraging them to compromise doctrinally. It was a movement of guile intended to bait or snare people together for the purpose of drawing a crowd. The seeds of this type of compromise are evident in many ecumenical gatherings today.

Essentially, the apostle is saying that the church at Thessalonica had integrity, as opposed to duplicity. It was evident that the Thessalonican believers assembled for the purpose of preaching the Gospel and giving Christ pre-eminence. In 2 Timothy 3:10, Paul said, *"But thou hast fully known my doctrine, manner of life, purpose, faith, longsuffering, charity, patience,"*

Years ago, the Lord called my dear friend, Dr. Curtis Hutson, home after a long battle with cancer. Dr. Hutson wrote me many letters in the final days of his life. One letter stated:

> I don't know how much longer I have for this world. The doctor does not hold out much hope for me; however, life and death are in the hands of the Lord, not medical science.
>
> I challenge you to take your place in the long line of independent, fundamental Baptists, who have stood for separation and soulwinning. I speak, now, especially of ecclesiastical separation. Hold that banner high until Jesus comes.

Dr. Hutson was admonishing and encouraging me to beware of deceitful gatherings that drop doctrinal distinctives for the purpose of gathering a crowd.

As Paul speaks of the motives of his ministry, we notice, also, that they were not man-centered.

But as we were allowed of God to be put in trust with the gospel, even so we speak; not as pleasing men, but God, which trieth our hearts. For neither at any time

used we flattering words, as ye know, nor a cloke
of covetousness; God is witness: Nor of men sought
we glory, neither of you, nor yet of others, when we
might have been burdensome, as the apostles of Christ.
—1 THESSALONIANS 2:4–6

The Laodicean churches of our day have unashamedly tailored their ministries after the desires of men. Seminars are given in which pastors are taught how to please men in the services.

I'm certainly not opposed to helping unregenerate men understand Bible words. I have challenged fundamental pastors in our day to make sure that our messages are clearly defined and easily understood. I believe the Bible is relevant and that a Spirit-filled preacher must be aware of the scriptural understanding, or lack thereof, of the congregation to whom he speaks. However, this awareness is not necessary in order to make the message more palatable. It is necessary to make the message understandable.

A popular concept that has been taught for nearly twenty years is that of surveying your community and asking people what type of church they would like to have in their community. Then, the church growth experts tell us to create a church that reflects the marketing analysis and the demographics of the area. It is my firm conviction that we, as pastors and Christian workers, must survey the book of Acts, determine the type of church that Jesus desires in our community, and then go out and give that type of church to the community for God's glory.

I once heard the story of a trip taken by Mohammed Ali to the Philippines in the height of his boxing career. As he sat down on a 747 airplane, the airplane soon began to taxi and prepare for takeoff. A flight attendant walked by and noticed that Ali did not have on his seat belt. She said, "Please fasten your seat belt, sir." He looked up proudly and snapped at her, "Superman don't need no seat belt, lady!" Without hesitation, she stared at him and said, "Superman don't need no airplane. Now buckle up!"

Today's lukewarm Christian, and the average unregenerate man, is boldly telling God's men what they do and do not want in church. We need preachers who will, lovingly, challenge our generation to follow God, even when it is not convenient to their flesh.

Galatians 1:10 says, *"For do I now persuade men, or God? or do I seek to please men? for if I yet pleased men, I should not be the servant of Christ."* Paul knew his target audience was God Himself. He was not as concerned about pleasing men as he was about pleasing God. Paul knew that he had been entrusted with the Gospel and intended to be a faithful servant, spreading the message of Christ.

It is not the business of the church to adapt Christ to men, but men to Christ. We must never forget our calling to bring men and women to the Saviour.

THE REDEFINING OF GRACE

Often, in the attempt of today's Laodicean church to please men, they have polluted the doctrine of grace. Somehow, an entire generation of Christians are being raised to believe that grace produces less holiness in the Christian life. In Titus 2:11–12,

Paul wrote, *"For the grace of God that bringeth salvation hath appeared to all men, Teaching us that, denying ungodliness and worldly lusts, we should live soberly, righteously, and godly, in this present world."* Someone who is growing in grace will not live a life that reflects less of God or His love, or a life that gives less to the work of the Lord.

In Galatians 5:13, Paul wrote, *"For, brethren, ye have been called unto liberty; only use not liberty for an occasion to the flesh, but by love serve one another."* Today, many Christians and pastors will argue that because they are under "grace" or "liberty," they can live, seemingly, without restraints.

It is our strong conviction that someone who is under grace will find himself growing, and *"so much the more as we see the day approaching."* It is our conviction that we will not serve or give less under grace, but that we will grow under grace.

I have often heard Christians say, "I am under grace. I can watch R-rated movies all day long if I want to."

"I am under grace. I can drink with my buddies if I want to."

But I have rarely heard anyone say, "I am under grace. Therefore, I am going to Africa as a missionary."

"Because I am under grace, I am giving my motor home as a part of a building offering."

This new brand of grace, that is being preached in the Laodicean churches today, is leading people to believe that they can live however they want to live, and it is all right with God.

Even as I write this, I know there will be some who feel that we are advocating some form of harsh legalism. That is not the case at all. We are advocating true grace. True grace will lead men and women to live *"soberly, righteously and godly in this present world."*

We have no desire to see people merely conform to an outward standard, but have a strong desire to see men and women grow in the grace and knowledge of our Lord Jesus Christ to the point that they will be conformed to His image.

May God give us pastors today who are not market-driven but Spirit-lead. May we be reminded that the church is not man's but the Lord's. Acts 20:28 says, *"Take heed therefore unto yourselves, and to all the flock, over the which the Holy Ghost hath made you overseers, to feed the church of God, which he hath purchased with his own blood."* Surely, He has purchased it with His own blood.

In Spurgeon's monthly magazine, *The Sword and the Trowel*, an anonymous article noted the tendency to drift away from sound doctrine. The author likened this drifting from truth to a downhill slope and thus labeled it the "downgrade." The inroads of modernism into the church later killed 90% of the main line denominations within a generation of Spurgeon's death. Spurgeon, once the celebrated and adored herald of the Baptist Union, was marginalized by the society and eventually withdrew his membership. His desire was simply to help avoid a downgrade. But the spirit of his age literally led to the deaths of many of the churches in England a century later. Could the same spirit in our day cause many churches to become so much like the world that one hundred years from now they will not even be noticeable as churches?

Paul's motives, in every area, were right and pure. He was not deceitful, man-centered or covetous in his ministry. There was no pretext for greed in what he was saying or doing. It was all for the glory of God.

PERSONAL CARE AND A POWERFUL MESSAGE

The second great characteristic of the church at Thessalonica was that it was a church with a personal ministry. The Apostle Paul was very personal in his care of the Christians. In 1 Thessalonians 2:7, the Bible states: *"But we were gentle among you, even as a nurse cherisheth her children."*

Notice that he was gentle amongst the people. We, as Bible-believing Christians, must maintain a strong position doctrinally. Our convictions will be challenged, but we must stay grounded in the Word of God. We also, however, must be gentle and easily approached, by the lost and by the new believers with whom we minister. Jude said, in verse 22, *"And of some have compassion, making a difference."*

While preaching recently to a group of several hundred pastors and Christian workers in Australia, a man approached me during the intermission. The man's name was Wai. He told me that some of the things I had said were convicting to him. In the course of the conversation, I felt led to ask Wai if he had ever accepted Jesus Christ as his personal Saviour. As it turned out, Wai was a governmental leader from the country of Papua New Guinea. He had attended the conference with missionary Gary Keck. Gary and others had been witnessing to him and brought him to the conference with hopes that he might further understand Christianity.

I took Wai into a side office and began to share with him the love of Christ. Although he felt conviction for his sin because of a message I had preached about the Christian family, I did not condemn him for his shortcomings, sins and failures. I simply showed him the love of Christ and the way of salvation. After a few moments, Wai prayed to accept Jesus Christ as Saviour. I thank the Lord that, somehow through the message, Wai not only sensed the strength of our convictions, but also our hearts of concern for him.

This is further emphasized when Paul speaks of the necessity of being patient in the ministry. New Christians in this post-modern society need to know that, while we will not change our stand, we will lovingly nurture them where they are spiritually to help them grow in Christ.

Not only was the Apostle Paul personal in his care, but he was also personal in his commitment to the people. First Thessalonians 2:8 says, *"So being affectionately desirous of you, we were willing to have imparted unto you, not the gospel of God only, but also our own souls, because ye were dear unto us."*

People do not care how much we know until they know how much we care. Paul gave the true Gospel with an affectionate presentation. His heart and spirit were stirred within him as he visited cities like Athens that were given totally to idolatry.

A POWERFUL MESSAGE

The Saviour-sensitive church will not only be one with pure motives and a personalized ministry, but most importantly, it will be one with a powerful message. Thank God that there is still power in His preserved Word.

First Thessalonians 2:13 says, *"For this cause also thank we God without ceasing, because, when ye received the word of God which ye heard of us, ye received it not as the word of men, but as it is in truth, the word of God, which effectually worketh also in you that believe."* Paul clearly states that the epistle he was writing was given to him by direct revelation. This was not his opinion and these were not his ideas. This was the very Word of God. Thank God that we too can receive the Bible as the very Word of God.

First Peter 1:23 says, *"Being born again, not of corruptible seed, but of incorruptible, by the word of God, which liveth and abideth for ever."* Matthew 4:4 says, *"But he answered and said, It is written, Man shall not live by bread alone, but by every word that proceedeth out of the mouth of God."*

Not only does power exist in the preserved Word of God, but it also exists in the preached Word of God. First Thessalonians 2:9 says, *"For ye remember, brethren, our labour and travail: for labouring night and day, because we would not be chargeable unto any of you, we preached unto you the gospel of God."* Notice Paul emphasized the preaching of the Gospel.

First Timothy 3:16 says, *"And without controversy great is the mystery of godliness: God was manifest in the flesh, justified in the Spirit, seen of angels, preached unto the Gentiles, believed on in the world, received up into glory."* How we thank God for the wonderful mystery of the Gospel, which has been revealed to all men.

This is why the Holy Spirit led Paul to write Romans 1:16, *"For I am not ashamed of the gospel of Christ: for it is the power of God unto salvation to every one that believeth; to the Jew first, and also to the Greek."* We must come back to the conviction that it is the Gospel, alone, that will draw men to the Saviour and bring true spiritual results in the church.

Several church growth, seeker-sensitive leaders of this generation have stated that modern-day Pharisees are more concerned about *purity* than *people*. We are convinced that there must be concern on both counts. Jesus was concerned for people, but He was also concerned about purity. Ephesians 5:27 says, *"That he might present it to himself a glorious church, not having spot, or wrinkle, or any such thing; but that it should be holy and without blemish."*

The local church is to be the pillar and the ground of Truth. We must be concerned about doctrinal purity. At the same time, the Son of man has come to seek and to save the lost. We must continually be concerned for people. A so-called love for people that presents a message of psycho babble and diluted truth is not truly a love for people at all.

We have personally met dozens of people who are comfortable in the seeker-sensitive environment and feel accepted as people, yet have never trusted Christ as Saviour.

Recently, while helping my son purchase a car, we began speaking to the sales manager of a large Ford dealership here in southern California. He told me about the church he attends and how he loves the music and the way they "rock out." He shared with me that he felt the messages were interesting. He had attended most Sundays for the past two years. When I asked him if he knew he was on his way to Heaven eternally and had ever accepted Christ as Saviour, he said, "The thing I like about the church I attend is that they really don't pressure me into any particular decision." Can we really say that we are concerned about people when we do not confront them with their need for Christ?

Second Timothy 4:1–4 gives a charge to every true man of God. This charge states:

> *I charge thee therefore before God, and the Lord Jesus Christ, who shall judge the quick and the dead at his appearing and his kingdom; Preach the word; be instant in season, out of season; reprove, rebuke, exhort with all longsuffering and doctrine. For the time will come when they will not endure sound doctrine; but after their own lusts shall they heap to themselves teachers, having itching ears; And they shall turn away their ears from the truth, and shall be turned unto fables.*

Some of the more caustic seeker-sensitive leaders literally ridicule preaching. Advertisements have been placed in large city newspapers with a "Billy Sunday" type of figure, pointing his finger and preaching from a pulpit. The newspaper advertisement says, "If you're tired of this, come to our church this Sunday."

Now, the questions must be asked, "Have there been churches with a fundamental position that have been uncaring or have experienced some type of failure that has brought shame to the cause of Christ? Have there been caustic pulpits in our fundamental movement?" The answer is "Yes." But do we throw away the baby with the bath water? Do we stop preaching a strong, uncompromising message because of a few failures or because people simply don't like preaching anymore?

I am afraid that entertainment has hijacked many pulpits across the country. Everyone seems to want revival without prayer, preaching or consecration.

The preaching of the Word of God is an authoritative declaration of the truth of God's Word. Starving men do not need road shows in church. They need a table full of Christ.

Recently, my wife and I were out visiting folks on a Saturday morning. We were able to visit the widow of our former state senator, Pete Knight. Pete was a decorated Vietnam veteran, a test pilot, an astronaut, and later served our community in Sacramento.

After a battle with cancer, he passed away recently, so Terrie and I wanted to visit his wife and offer some encouragement and comfort to her. In the process of speaking to her in her home, she shared with us that she had a Catholic background. She said, "The one thing about the messages at your church is that they were always about Christ." I had the opportunity to ask Gail if she knew Christ personally, and if she would spend eternity in Heaven. After a few moments of sharing the Scriptures, Gail prayed to receive Jesus Christ as Saviour.

Do we love Gail Knight? Yes! And, because of our love for her, we could not hide the truth about Christ.

Every time we stand to preach or go out into the community with the Gospel, we run the risk of offending people. The Apostle Paul not only offended people, he suffered the consequences of those offences in nearly every one of his stops along the way of his missionary journeys.

Going back to the church of Laodicea, we find one of the saddest portions of Scripture in the Bible. Revelation 3:20 tells us that Jesus is standing at the door of the church, knocking. While there may be a soulwinning application to this verse, Revelation 3:20 is speaking about Jesus standing outside the door of the church of Laodicea, wanting to come in. Unfortunately, however, the church felt that they were rich, increased with goods and did not need the Lord. They did not realize that, from God's perspective, they were poor and blind. They did not realize how desperately they needed Him. They were no longer sensitive to Him. They were merely sensitive to what they wanted and to what the people in their community wanted.

May God help us to truly consider the issues at hand today. May we recognize the necessity of being sensitive to the Saviour and be willing to stand for the Truth in this needy hour.

I pray that our church will proclaim God's Word and will reflect this renewed sensitivity to Him. May we, once again, see a true revival of repentance in our own hearts, in our churches and throughout our country.

A PORTRAIT OF THE SAVIOUR-SENSITIVE CHURCH

EXCERPT FROM **THE SAVIOUR SENSITIVE CHURCH**
BY DR. PAUL CHAPPELL AND DR. JOHN GOETSCH

THE PHILOSOPHY OF A SAVIOUR-SENSITIVE CHURCH

For years, there has been a growing movement in our country called the seeker-sensitive church movement. Many churches, including independent Baptist churches, have been influenced by a philosophy that is very man-centered, as opposed to being God-centered. Many pastors are buying into the post-modern thought of our day and leading their churches down a path of pragmatism and carnality.

These churches are not based upon the unchanging Word of God, but are rather structured and restructured constantly to appease the appetites of men. These churches have cast off the authority of God's truth and have shouldered the mantle of designer truth, as mentioned in section one.

It has never been easy to stand and "speak the truth in love." Yet, it has never been more necessary than in the day in which we live.

> *And unto the angel of the church of the Laodiceans write; These things saith the Amen, the faithful and true witness, the beginning of the creation of God; I know thy works, that thou art neither cold nor hot: I would thou wert cold or hot. So then because thou art lukewarm, and neither cold nor hot, I will spue thee out of my mouth. Because thou sayest, I am rich, and increased with goods, and have need of nothing; and knowest not that thou art wretched, and miserable, and poor, and blind, and naked: I counsel thee to buy of me gold tried in the fire, that thou mayest be rich; and white raiment, that thou mayest be clothed, and that the shame of thy nakedness do not appear; and anoint thine eyes with eyesalve, that thou mayest see. As many as I love, I rebuke and chasten: be zealous therefore, and repent. Behold, I stand at the door, and knock: if any man hear my voice, and open the door, I will come in to him, and will sup with him, and he with me.*
> —REVELATION 3:14–20

Some of the saddest words in all of the Bible to me are the words, "*Behold, I stand at the door, and knock: if any man hear my voice, and open the door, I will come in to him, and will sup with him, and he with me.*" The reason these words are sad to me is because this verse tells us that Jesus Christ was literally knocking on the door of the Laodicean church–pushed out of His own church and not allowed inside!

Our goal in church ministry should always be to please Christ and to glorify Him in the church. Second Timothy 2:3–4 teaches, "*Thou therefore endure hardness, as a good soldier of Jesus Christ. No man that warreth entangleth himself with the affairs of this life; that he may please him who hath chosen him to be a soldier.*" Thus, our goal is not to please a group, a denomination, or the unregenerate men and women living in our community. Our goal is not to please men or attract a crowd. Ephesians 6:6–7 says, "*Not with eyeservice, as menpleasers; but as the servants of Christ, doing the will of God from the heart; With good will doing service, as to the Lord, and not to men.*"

Our desire, as pastors must be first and foremost that our churches would be Saviour-sensitive in every way—giving Christ the preeminence in all things. Colossians 1:17–19, "*And he is before all things, and by him all things consist. And he is the head of the body, the church: who is the beginning, the firstborn from the dead; that in all things he might have the preeminence. For it pleased the Father that in him should all fulness dwell.*"

In this section, I want to explore with you the philosophy, the practice, and the price associated with growing a true, Saviour-sensitive church. In these chapters, we will see ten defining characteristics found in a church that places Christ at the head. Let's first explore the philosophy—the functional foundation of a church that seeks to please Christ above all.

THE OWNERSHIP OF THE
SAVIOUR-SENSITIVE CHURCH

The seeker-sensitive movement has taken the authority of the church and placed it into the hands of the community at large. Pastors are taking community surveys regarding musical tastes, sermon content, service stylings, and even whether or not to use Bible words such as *sin* or *hell*. Many supposed gatherings of Christians have even removed the name "church" in an attempt to blend in with the community and appeal to the lost.

Friend, the problem with this is that a Saviour-sensitive church is not "the people's church" but it truly is the Lord's church. The Bible speaks to pastors in 1 Peter 5 challenging them to be overseers of the flock. Yet, 1 Peter 5:3 says, "*Neither as being lords over God's heritage, but being ensamples to the flock.*" Here we see the church is the Lord's heritage. In fact, Acts 20:28 states, "*Take heed therefore unto yourselves, and to all the flock, over the which the Holy Ghost hath made you overseers, to feed the church of God, which he hath purchased with his own blood.*" The church does not belong to the people, the community, the pastor, or even the church family. The church belongs to Jesus Christ! The true, local New Testament church is an institution that Jesus Christ gave His own life to purchase unto Himself.

> *For the husband is the head of the wife, even as Christ is the head of the church: and he is the saviour of the body. Therefore as the church is subject unto Christ, so let the wives be to their own husbands in every thing. Husbands, love your wives, even as Christ also loved the church, and gave himself for it; That he might sanctify and cleanse it with the washing of water by the*

word, That he might present it to himself a glorious church, not having spot, or wrinkle, or any such thing; but that it should be holy and without blemish.
—EPHESIANS 5:23–27

The very root problem in modern-day church compromise is the question of authority. Christ is no longer the owner and His Word is no longer the final authority. At the heart of a Saviour-sensitive church, the pastor and the people have a deeply held understanding that Christ is the head. They submit themselves in mutual accountability and submission to the authority of His Word in all matters of faith and practice. In this kind of church, the pastor and people must die to self-will and fleshly desire and must live in constant submission to doing God's work God's way.

THE MESSAGE OF THE SAVIOUR-SENSITIVE CHURCH

The message of the Saviour-sensitive church must always be biblical in its content. It must not merely be a message of psychology or man's thoughts with a few verses supporting what a man wants to say.

I charge thee therefore before God, and the Lord Jesus Christ, who shall judge the quick and the dead at his appearing and his kingdom; Preach the word; be instant in season, out of season; reprove, rebuke, exhort with all longsuffering and doctrine. For the time will come when they will not endure sound doctrine; but after their own lusts shall they heap to themselves teachers,

having itching ears; And they shall turn away their
ears from the truth, and shall be turned unto fables.
—2 TIMOTHY 4:1–4

Notice the Bible says, "*For the time will come when they*
will not endure sound doctrine; but after their own lusts shall they
heap to themselves teachers, having itching ears." There are many
teachers today who are willing to say whatever people want to
hear—whatever keeps donors happy and airtime paid for!

The Saviour-sensitive church, however, will not change
the message to please men. At times, the message will be
confrontational. At times biblical words may need to be defined
and explained. At times the truth will pierce and prod–bringing
the sting of conviction. This was the case when Jesus met the
woman at the well in John 4.

At Lancaster Baptist Church we have never apologized for
preaching truth that is confrontational, but we also endeavor
to make the message understandable. For example, we define
doctrinal terms from our pulpit and illustrate with various
visuals, but we will never change the message in an effort to
make it more palatable or more tolerable—to tickle the ears. We
will not remove distasteful portions of the Scripture simply to
please the society in which we live.

The Word of God is powerful and must be preached with
conviction. It must be declared with authority and it must be
central to every message and every Sunday school lesson. Paul
said in Romans 1:14–16,

I am debtor both to the Greeks, and to the Barbarians;
both to the wise, and to the unwise. So, as much as in

me is, I am ready to preach the gospel to you that are at Rome also. For I am not ashamed of the gospel of Christ: for it is the power of God unto salvation to every one that believeth; to the Jew first, and also to the Greek.

God said in Jeremiah 3:15, *"And I will give you pastors according to mine heart, which shall feed you with knowledge and understanding."* Again God refers to preaching in 1 Corinthians 1:18–21,

For the preaching of the cross is to them that perish foolishness; but unto us which are saved it is the power of God. For it is written, I will destroy the wisdom of the wise, and will bring to nothing the understanding of the prudent. Where is the wise? where is the scribe? where is the disputer of this world? hath not God made foolish the wisdom of this world? For after that in the wisdom of God the world by wisdom knew not God, it pleased God by the foolishness of preaching to save them that believe.

The message of the Saviour-sensitive church must continually lift up the Cross, the Gospel of Jesus Christ, and the life-changing truth of God's Word.

THE MISSION OF THE SAVIOUR-SENSITIVE CHURCH

A Saviour-sensitive church has a two-fold mission. The first relates to the function of the Holy Spirit, and the second relates to the great commission of Jesus Christ.

First, a Saviour-sensitive church's primary goal and mission is a desire to be sensitive to the Lord in all it does. First Thessalonians 5:19 says, "*Quench not the Spirit.*" A Saviour-sensitive Christian is someone who is yielded to the Holy Spirit. Titus 2:11–13 teaches, "*For the grace of God that bringeth salvation hath appeared to all men, Teaching us that, denying ungodliness and worldly lusts, we should live soberly, righteously, and godly, in this present world; Looking for that blessed hope, and the glorious appearing of the great God and our Saviour Jesus Christ.*"

A Christian, growing in the grace and knowledge of our Lord Jesus Christ, will not speak of grace and liberty as an occasion to the flesh but will realize that the grace of God is the inner working of the Holy Spirit, bringing him or her into the image of Jesus Christ.

In his book *The Discipline of Grace*, Jerry Bridges says, "There has been a reaction to 'legalism'—but we need to watch that in our assertion of freedom, we do not give the flesh the opportunity to lead us over the precipice into sin."[1]

Many Christians in this day are so sensitive to their own perceived needs that they have given in to an accommodating style of theology in which they manipulate the Bible to say what they want rather than rightly dividing the Word of Truth. If we will be a Saviour-sensitive church, we must be sensitive to the Saviour and to the inner working of His Holy Spirit.

Second, the church must also be sensitive to the mission of the Lord Jesus Christ. In Matthew 28:19–20, Jesus was very clear when He said, "*Go ye therefore, and teach all nations, baptizing*

---

1.   Jerry Bridges, *The Discipline of Grace* (Colorado: NavPress, 1994)

them in the name of the Father, and of the Son, and of the Holy Ghost: Teaching them to observe all things whatsoever I have commanded you: and, lo, I am with you alway, even unto the end of the world. Amen." Additionally, Luke 19:10 says, *"For the Son of man is come to seek and to save that which was lost."*

The mission of Jesus Christ was to seek and to save the lost. The mission He gave us before He ascended to Heaven was to reach the whole world with the Gospel. Some churches today literally target a mere segment of the society—the yuppies, the high income earners, etc. Many seminars even teach pastors how to market their churches for a certain income level in their community.

The mission Jesus gave the church never drew such lines! The Gospel message should be taken to every single person in your community. This is what the Saviour did, and this is what a Saviour-sensitive church will do as well!

THE MOTIVATION OF THE SAVIOUR-SENSITIVE CHURCH

It is obvious that the church at Laodicea was motivated by its own selfish desires. They were the church "of the Laodiceans." This church left Jesus outside, standing at the door, wanting to come in. What should motivate the church that is seeking to be sensitive to the Saviour?

The first motivation must be the Word of God. The Scriptures teach that the local church is to be the pillar and the ground of truth. First Timothy 3:15 says, *"But if I tarry long, that thou mayest know how thou oughtest to behave thyself in the house of God, which is the church of the living God, the pillar and ground of the truth."*

A Saviour-sensitive church will be strongly motivated to protect and keep the Word of God—to lift it up, proclaim it, live it, preach it, and honor it. The Word of God will serve as the final authority—the framework of doctrine and the glue of common belief that holds the church family together in faith.

Second, a Saviour-sensitive church must be motivated by the love of Christ. Second Corinthians 5:14 says, *"For the love of Christ constraineth us; because we thus judge, that if one died for all, then were all dead:"* It is my prayer that not one person in our church would serve in a class, the choir, or any other ministry because of a mere sense of obligation. The overwhelming force constraining us to serve Christ must simply be the fact that we love Christ and want to serve Him.

The third motivation in a Saviour-sensitive church is the grace of God. Grace is a disposition created by the Holy Spirit of God. There are at least fifteen ways that we are motivated by the grace of God and through the Holy Spirit. We are motivated to serve God and one another, *"For, brethren, ye have been called unto liberty; only use not liberty for an occasion to the flesh, but by love serve one another"* (Galatians 5:13). We are motivated to encourage one another, *"Let no corrupt communication proceed out of your mouth, but that which is good to the use of edifying, that it may minister grace unto the hearers"* (Ephesians 4:29). We are motivated to give, *"Insomuch that we desired Titus, that as he had begun, so he would also finish in you the same grace also. Therefore, as ye abound in every thing, in faith, and utterance, and knowledge, and in all diligence, and in your love to us, see that ye abound in this grace also"* (2 Corinthians 8:6–7).

The grace of God at work in our hearts will do more to help us stay faithful to Christ than any other thing! Man-made "guilt trips," sensational dramas or films, high-power marketing ploys, and promotional gimmicks can never create within a church family the kind of love, devotion, commitment, and service that the incredible grace of God can produce!

THE PRACTICE OF A SAVIOUR-SENSITIVE CHURCH

What does a Saviour-sensitive church look like, practically speaking? In a day when almost anything goes in the name of God and religion, and when you can find "Burger King: have it your way" Christianity in every city, what does a true Bible-based church look like?

Interestingly, there are three major visible areas that seem to slip first in most seeker-sensitive churches. It seems that no matter the denomination or locale, the seeker-sensitive church movement is following the world as closely as possible in three major areas—the music, the youth, and the methods.

Let's take a close look at these three areas and what God teaches about His design and desire for the local church.

THE MUSIC OF THE SAVIOUR-SENSITIVE CHURCH

Time and space do not permit lengthy discussions about music in this text. The conscience of a Saviour-sensitive Christian—a

Holy Spirit-led believer—will bear witness against the CCM movement and will encourage the believer to find a church that does not seek to conform to this world.

Needless to say, the Scriptures teach us that we are to worship with psalms, hymns, and spiritual songs. Ephesians 5:18–20 is one of several passage that teaches this, *"And be not drunk with wine, wherein is excess; but be filled with the Spirit; Speaking to yourselves in psalms and hymns and spiritual songs, singing and making melody in your heart to the Lord; Giving thanks always for all things unto God and the Father in the name of our Lord Jesus Christ."*

The music in a Saviour-sensitive church does not focus on the musician. For eighteen years I have stated: "I do not want singers in our church who sing about the untold millions and yet never tell one person about Jesus Christ." We need musicians who truly live the Christian life and are not merely involved in entertainment.

Much of the pop-culture music of our day focuses strictly on the musician as an entertainer, and this philosophy has crept into seeker-sensitive churches as well.

Furthermore, the music in a Saviour-sensitive church does not focus on what the people want to hear or what the unsaved man wants to hear. Again, the focal point of our worship is the Lord Jesus Christ, Himself. Many churches have become so "market" or "culture" driven that they are now adapting to any and all kinds of music in an effort to "reach the world." This philosophy completely neglects the inherent power of music without words to evoke a godly or an ungodly response in the heart of a believer.

In recent days, a few authors of well-known books have stated that music is "amoral." I believe, however, that certain types of music most certainly appeal to the flesh and will draw men away from a godly and spiritual desire to worship the Lord. The term "spiritual songs" is from the Greek word *pneumatikos* which helps us realize that this is Holy Spirit given music. It cannot appeal to the flesh and to the Holy Spirit at the same time.

Music is not amoral. Every style of music without words provokes a spiritual response either toward or away from God. We cannot expect spiritual fruit to result when we bring the world's music into our church services. Churches by the thousands are incorporating carnal music into their "worship" in an effort to please men and draw crowds. Guess what? It's working! But that doesn't mean it is pleasing Christ, and it doesn't mean it's changing lives.

A Saviour-sensitive church must not be afraid of being perceived as a church with a different or traditional worship style. We must remember the words of Jeremiah the prophet in Jeremiah 10:2, "*Thus saith the LORD, Learn not the way of the heathen, and be not dismayed at the signs of heaven; for the heathen are dismayed at them.*"

Conforming to the world–musically or any other way—is the quickest way to "not reach the world." Why should the world want Christ, if Christ is no different from the world?

The music of a Saviour-sensitive church will always draw the hearts of both saved and lost men away from the world and toward the Saviour. It's that simple. In many churches, the drum set, the band, the performers simply mimic the world—and that rather poorly! The world doesn't need a cheaply reproduced late night talk show on Sunday morning. The world needs to see Christ, high and lifted up—holy!

In an effort to attract people with ungodly music, we distance them from God and defile His church with carnality. Spirit-led, Spirit-filled music will always be greatly different from the world and will in no way mimic or reproduce a secular style or feel. It will minister grace to the heart and draw the lost to new life in Christ!

> *I waited patiently for the Lord; and he inclined unto me, and heard my cry. He brought me up also out of an horrible pit, out of the miry clay, and set my feet upon a rock, and established my goings. And he hath put a new song in my mouth, even praise unto our God: many shall see it, and fear, and shall trust in the Lord.*—PSALM 40:1–3

> *I beseech you therefore, brethren, by the mercies of God, that ye present your bodies a living sacrifice, holy, acceptable unto God, which is your reasonable service. And be not conformed to this world: but be ye transformed by the renewing of your mind, that ye may prove what is that good, and acceptable, and perfect, will of God.*—ROMANS 12:1–2

THE METHODS OF THE SAVIOUR-SENSITIVE CHURCH

It is important to remember the phrase, "What we win them with is what we must keep them with." The methodology of the church should be biblically sound. Our message should be in agreement with the Scriptures and, in fact, they should come from the Scriptures. This is why at Lancaster Baptist Church, we still go out into the community and knock on doors, support missionaries, have special offerings, have godly women teaching the younger women, etc. Our methods are Bible-based and we must continue doing our best to follow God's blue-print (the Bible) as we serve Him.

As a side note, there are many good, sound, fundamental churches that will use slightly differing methods, yet they are methods that still fit within a biblical context. We must not be the type of insecure people who criticize a good, solid, fundamental church that may do some things a little differently (e.g. mid-week service on a different night, or a building that has a different architectural style, etc.).

As long as someone holds to sound doctrine and is endeavoring to win the lost to Jesus Christ, our spirit should be to praise God for souls that are being saved here at Lancaster Baptist as well as in other ministries.

THE YOUTH OF THE SAVIOUR-SENSITIVE CHURCH

One of my greatest concerns for teenagers growing up in the seeker-sensitive movement is that they are seeing a watered-down concept of what Christianity truly is. They are watching their churches change before their very eyes. They see their pastors removing the pulpits and sitting on stools, removing the choirs and implementing "wanna-be" rock bands. The teenagers, in many cases, are following this example, and thus Christianity gets farther and farther from what it truly was in the New Testament.

Further, I am concerned that teenagers growing up in these types of churches will get the idea that church is about them and not about the Lord. I am convinced that many of the churches that are now joining together and emphasizing the seeker-sensitive philosophy will find that their young people will not be called to preach or to go to the mission field. They will not be attending Bible college, and many of the Bible colleges who fellowship with seeker-sensitive churches will change more and more to liberal arts programs, as they seek to accommodate the very churches that fed them with students.

If these children are growing up in a seeker-sensitive environment, where church is all about "them," why would they consider "abandoning self" or "dying to self?" Why would they want to take up their cross and truly follow Christ?

Conversely, teenagers in the Saviour-sensitive church will see godly mentors. Philippians 4:9 says, "*Those things, which ye have both learned, and received, and heard, and seen in me, do: and the God of peace shall be with you.*" We need mentors who will be able to say, "Do what you see in me." We need teenagers who will have youth pastors who emphasize a godly and holy lifestyle, who show them how to win others to Christ, and who model a faithful, separated life in the ministry.

I thank God for our youth pastors who are tremendous mentors for our young people. I believe it is because of the parents of our church, who have cooperated with our youth pastors, that many of our young people are serving God with their lives—both in and out of full-time ministry.

THE COST OF A SAVIOUR-SENSITIVE MINISTRY

There will always be a cost in maintaining a Saviour-sensitive ministry. Some Christians, who are part of the Laodicean seeker movement, will claim that a church which stays doctrinally and practically in the position which they once held, is one that does not emphasize grace. They will claim that we are legalistic, or that we emphasize doctrine over the needs of the people.

A mature believer realizes that "standards" should never be the ultimate goal of a church. Jesus Christ is our goal. If we have a "standard" that is based on a Bible principle, and it has helped us in living the Christian life, then we have liberty to worship the Lord in that context.

Others will justify the path they have chosen by criticizing a church that will remain the same. This is a part of the cost of being a Saviour-sensitive ministry.

Not only will the seeker-sensitive type of Christians reject the philosophy of churches across America that are more conservative, but sometimes the things stated about more conservative churches will be less than kind. While the seeker-sensitive crowd may speak about grace, they often will show very little grace when speaking of Saviour-sensitive churches.

They often remind me of the politically liberal crowd in America who speak about tolerance but are very intolerant toward the religious right. So, the seeker-sensitive movement speaks about grace but shows little toward churches that choose to worship the Lord in a "more conservative" context.

In Ernest Pickering's booklet *Are Fundamentalists Legalists?* we read,

As we have seen, grace not only liberates from sin and its consequences, it also enslaves us to Christ and produces holiness of life. As believers, we must not only celebrate the liberation of grace, but also the purification of grace. The same grace which sets us free, also challenges us with high standards of living and, thankfully, enables us to reach them. *"Brethren, the grace of our Lord Jesus Christ be with your spirit"* (Galatians 6:18).[2]

Someone who is not interested in the purifying effects of grace, which causes us to serve the Lord more faithfully, may reject a Christian who is endeavoring to grow in grace biblically. Galatians 5:13 says, *"For, brethren, ye have been called unto liberty; only use not liberty for an occasion to the flesh, but by love serve one another."* May we allow the grace of God and the liberty He has given us to motivate us to serve our Lord Jesus Christ and one another.

THE ALTERNATIVE TO SAVIOUR-SENSITIVE MINISTRY

As I have mentioned previously, the alternative to seeking to please the Saviour is to seek to please the culture around us. Romans 12:1–2 says,

> *I beseech you therefore, brethren, by the mercies of God, that ye present your bodies a living sacrifice, holy, acceptable unto God, which is your reasonable*

---

2.   Enest Pickering, *Are Fundamentalists Legalists?* (Alabama: Baptist World Mission)

service. And be not conformed to this world: but be ye transformed by the renewing of your mind, that ye may prove what is that good, and acceptable, and perfect, will of God.

We must not desire to conform to the world's system but to maintain our stand as a distinctive Baptist church.

Frankly, one may wonder where the compromise will end. If churches and pastors continue to follow the pathway of post-modernism, if they continue to question and change the truth with their new philosophies, I am afraid to contemplate what "church" will look like twenty years from now. Already, many main-line denominations ordain homosexuals as pastors. Where will the seeker-sensitive concept stop?

THE REWARD OF THE SAVIOUR-SENSITIVE CHURCH

Finally, I want you to contemplate the reward of being faithful to the Saviour. The reward will be spiritual fruit. I believe that in our Bible-preaching churches across America in which the Gospel is preached faithfully, and men and women are called upon to turn to the Lord Jesus Christ for salvation, the fruit will truly be fruit brought about by the inner working of the Holy Spirit.

Not only do I believe that we will see fruit in the realm of souls being saved, but I also believe there will be eternal rewards for churches and Christians who remain faithful. In 1 Corinthians 3:11–15, the Scriptures say,

For other foundation can no man lay than that is laid, which is Jesus Christ. Now if any man build upon this foundation gold, silver, precious stones, wood, hay, stubble; Every man's work shall be made manifest: for the day shall declare it, because it shall be revealed by fire; and the fire shall try every man's work of what sort it is. If any man's work abide which he hath built thereupon, he shall receive a reward. If any man's work shall be burned, he shall suffer loss: but he himself shall be saved; yet so as by fire.

Much of what is being done today, in an effort to please men, will burn as wood, hay and stubble at the Judgment (Bema) Seat of Jesus Christ.

We may not always receive the rewards and appreciation we feel we deserve here on earth, but I truly believe the goal of the Saviour-sensitive church is, and should always be, that we would hear the Lord say, "Well done, thou good and faithful servant!"

Visit us online

strivingtogether.com

wcbc.edu

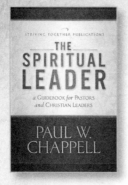
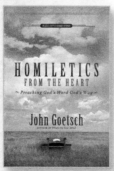
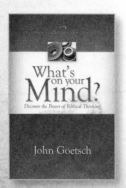

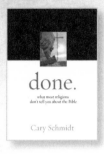

done.
Specifically created to be placed into the hands of an unsaved person and a perfect gift for first-time church visitors, this minibook explains the Gospel in crystal clear terms. The reader will journey step by step through biblical reasoning that concludes at the Cross and a moment of decision. This tool will empower your whole church family to share the Gospel with anyone! (100 pages, mini paperback)

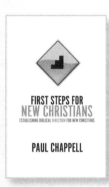

First Steps for New Christians
This resource is a powerful "pre-discipleship" tool that will help to quickly get a new convert on the path of growth and spiritual stability. It is perfect to use in alter packets or follow-up visits with new Christians and should be given to everyone your church family brings to Christ. (100 pages, paperback)

Daily in the Word
Third Edition
Daily in the Word is designed to be a journey in personal discipleship that leads every Christian to not only *be* a disciple, but to *make* disciples! It is written to be a one-on-one partnership with a discipler training a disciple who will then be able to train others. (128 pages, paperback)

strivingtogether.com